# WASHINGTON, D.C.
# GUIDEBOOK for KIDS

**A Fun Workbook That Guides Kids Through Our Nation's Capital**

By Carol Bluestone and Susan Irwin

# WASHINGTON, D.C.
# GUIDEBOOK FOR KIDS

By Carol Bluestone and Susan Irwin

Noodle Press
Washington, D.C.
Copyright © 1976, 1987 by Carol Bluestone and Susan Irwin
Revised 1987, 1988, 1990, 1992, 1995
First edition 1976

All rights reserved.

No part of this publication may be reproduced in any
form without the permission of Noodle Press.

Library of Congress Catalogue Number: 87-50322
ISBN: 0-9601022-4-8

Printed in USA

*Inquiries regarding bulk orders* for retail sales and for
classroom and organizational use should be addressed to:

Noodle Press
P.O. Box 42542
Washington, D.C. 20015

**For Zack and Gabe and all the
young visitors to our wonderful city**

Historical photos courtesy of Library of Congress
Engravings courtesy of Bureau of Engraving and Printing
Center map courtesy of National Park Service
Metro map courtesy of Metro
Book design by Minker Design, Bethesda, MD

# CONTENTS

### CHAPTER 1
**WELCOME TO WASHINGTON** . . . . . . . . . . .2
What Makes Washington Special . . . . . . . . .3
Find Out What's Happening . . . . . . . . . . . .4
How to Get Around . . . . . . . . . . . . . . . . . .5

### CHAPTER 2
**HOW THE CAPITAL WAS BORN** . . . . . . . . .7

### CHAPTER 3
**OUR WORKING GOVERNMENT** . . . . . . . . . 11
Bureau of Engraving and Printing . . . . . . . . 12
Capitol . . . . . . . . . . . . . . . . . . . . . . . . . . 13
Federal Bureau of Investigation (F.B.I.) . . . . . 16
Supreme Court . . . . . . . . . . . . . . . . . . . . 18
White House . . . . . . . . . . . . . . . . . . . . . . 20

### CHAPTER 4
**MONUMENTS AND MEMORIALS**
**Honoring Our History** . . . . . . . . . . . . . . . 24
Arlington National Cemetery. . . . . . . . . . . . 25
Kennedy Center for the Performing Arts . . . . 26
Lincoln Memorial. . . . . . . . . . . . . . . . . . . . 26
Marine Corps War Memorial (Iwo Jima Statue) 28
Thomas Jefferson Memorial. . . . . . . . . . . . . 28
Vietnam Veterans Memorial . . . . . . . . . . . . 30
Vietnam Women's Memorial. . . . . . . . . . . . 30
Washington Monument . . . . . . . . . . . . . . . 31

### CHAPTER 5
**HISTORIC HOUSES AND SITES**
**Preserving Our Past** . . . . . . . . . . . . . . . . .35
Alexandria, Virginia . . . . . . . . . . . . . . . . . .36
Arlington House . . . . . . . . . . . . . . . . . . . .37
Chesapeake & Ohio Canal (C & O Canal) . . .38
Clara Barton National Historic Site . . . . . . . .39
Ford's Theatre . . . . . . . . . . . . . . . . . . . . . 40
Frederick Douglass National Historic Site . . . 41
Georgetown . . . . . . . . . . . . . . . . . . . . . . 42
House Where Lincoln Died . . . . . . . . . . . . 40
Mount Vernon . . . . . . . . . . . . . . . . . . . . . 43
Woodlawn Plantation . . . . . . . . . . . . . . . .43

### CHAPTER 6
**MUSEUMS AND COLLECTIONS** . . . . . . . . . 44
Capital Children's Museum . . . . . . . . . . . . 45
Daughters of the American Revolution
    Museum . . . . . . . . . . . . . . . . . . . . . . 45
Holocaust Memorial Museum (United States) . 46
Library of Congress . . . . . . . . . . . . . . . . . 46
Marine Corps Museum. . . . . . . . . . . . . . . 50
National Archives . . . . . . . . . . . . . . . . . . 47
National Gallery of Art . . . . . . . . . . . . . . . 49
Navy Memorial and Visitors Center
    (United States) . . . . . . . . . . . . . . . . . . 50
Navy Museum . . . . . . . . . . . . . . . . . . . . 49
Smithsonian Institution . . . . . . . . . . . . . . . 50
    Anacostia Museum . . . . . . . . . . . . . . . 55
    Arthur M. Sackler Gallery . . . . . . . . . . . 55
    Arts and Industries Building . . . . . . . . . 54
    Freer Gallery. . . . . . . . . . . . . . . . . . . . 55
    Hirshhorn Museum and
        Sculpture Garden . . . . . . . . . . . . . . 51
    National Air and Space Museum . . . . . . 52
    National Museum of African Art. . . . . . . 55
    National Museum of American Art . . . . . 55
    National Museum of American History . . . . 53
    National Museum of Natural History . . . 54
    National Portrait Gallery . . . . . . . . . . . . 56
    National Postal Museum . . . . . . . . . . . 56
    Renwick Gallery . . . . . . . . . . . . . . . . . 57
Washington Dolls' House and Toy Museum. . . 57

### CHAPTER 7
**OUR NATURAL WORLD** . . . . . . . . . . . . . .58
Botanic Garden . . . . . . . . . . . . . . . . . . . .59
Great Falls Park . . . . . . . . . . . . . . . . . . . .60
National Aquarium . . . . . . . . . . . . . . . . . .60
National Arboretum . . . . . . . . . . . . . . . . .60
National Geographic (Explorers Hall) . . . . . .60
National Zoological Park (The Zoo) . . . . . . .61
Theodore Roosevelt Island . . . . . . . . . . . . .61

Washington, D.C. Map . . . . . . . . . . . . . .32–33
Answers to Quizzes and Puzzles . . . . . . . . . . 62
Metro Map . . . . . . . . . . . .Inside Back Cover

**CHAPTER 1**

# WELCOME TO WASHINGTON

*A U.S. Park policeman patrols the Mall*

**A** visit to Washington can be an exciting adventure — it's up to you. Is this your first trip to the capital, or have you been here before? Either way, this book is designed to be used by you, the young traveler. Even if you're a neighbor or native of the capital, this book will help you to explore and know your city better.

You'll find out lots of interesting facts about the major sights. (Did you know that during the Civil War the Capitol building was used as a hospital and a bakery?) You'll also find that there are many things to do in Washington just for fun or when you're tired of sightseeing. (How about a bike ride along the C & O Canal?) You'll also learn how to get around the city using public transportation.

You're going to find out how much you already know about Washington and its history AND how much more you'll know after your exploration. Games and puzzles are included for those in-between times when you just don't feel like taking another step. And when you're back home, this book will be a great souvenir of your trip.

Like any other place you may visit, there is more to a city than reading guidebooks and looking at buildings. Sometimes the most interesting things are those that you discover by yourself. When you visit special places, make sure that the front view of a building isn't all that you see. Look up at the rooftops and

# CHAPTER 1 – WELCOME TO WASHINGTON

between the buildings, or stand back and see how the buildings somehow fit together.

And don't just use your eyes when you're exploring — use your ears, your nose, your fingers, and your toes! Sounds and smells can tell you things that your eyes can't. Experiencing a city involves all of your senses.

## WHAT MAKES WASHINGTON SPECIAL

**W**hether you've arrived in Washington by car, train, plane, boat, (or even covered wagon), you are bound to notice that the city is different from any other you've ever seen. For example:

- **There are no skyscrapers and few buildings are taller than 130 feet**, so that the Capitol and the important monuments can be seen from as far away as possible.

- **There are many wide avenues and circles.** Many of the avenues and streets are named after states; and the circles, which have statues and fountains in the middle, are named after famous people.

- **There are few factories and smokestacks** since most of the people in Washington work in office buildings.

AND there are many differences which are not as easy to see.

- **Washington is a city without a state.** When George Washington picked out the land for the new nation's capital, he did not have in mind the creation of a new "state." Instead, the city became a federal district and that's why it's called the District of Columbia. As a result, Washington has no senators or congressmen. It only has a delegate to the House of Representatives, but he (or she) does not have the right to vote like the congressmen.

- **More than one hundred foreign nations have embassies in Washington.** Each embassy is a building owned by a different country. These countries send people, called diplomats and ambassadors, to the capital to represent them in the United States. You can see many of these beautiful embassies along a part of Massachusetts Avenue above Dupont Circle. This section is often referred to as

## CHAPTER 1—WELCOME TO WASHINGTON

"Embassy Row." Look for the flags and seals of the foreign countries on the fronts of these buildings.

★ **The United States government is the largest employer in Washington.** As the nation has grown in size and importance, more and more people have been needed to help run the country. In the last sixty years alone, the population of the Washington area has grown from about one million people to over three million. Hundreds of thousands of these people work in the large buildings which line the streets of downtown Washington. Look at the names on these buildings — "Treasury Department," "State Department," "Federal Trade Commission." Every day they are filled with people who are helping to make our government work.

★ **Many people live in Washington for only a few years.** Every time a new president is elected, he brings new people to Washington to work for him. Many of those who worked for the former president leave the city. That's why when Washingtonians meet each other, the first questions they ask are, "Where are you from?" and "How long have you lived here?"

★ **Thousands of organizations have offices in Washington.** In fact, probably every major group in the entire country is represented. National headquarters of the 4-H Clubs are here, and so are people representing churches, teachers, farmers, environmentalists, and almost any other group you can think of.

So, as you can see, Washington is unique in a number of ways. The personality of the city also includes the busy crowds in Georgetown on a Saturday afternoon, the glamour of a new play at the National Theater, and the excitement of world events happening around the corner.

## FIND OUT WHAT'S HAPPENING

**B**efore starting out, it's a good idea to check for events that are going on around town. There may be special exhibits and programs at the museums; there may be concerts, puppet shows, and festivals going on at nearby parks and theaters.

These sources have up-to-the minute information on events:

★ *Washington Post* "Carousel," in Friday's Weekend section.

★ *Washingtonian* Magazine, "Where and When."

★ " Kiosk," a calendar of National Park Service events, available at the monuments and on the Mall.

★ Call (202) 789-7000 for Washington Visitor Information Center located at 1455 Pennsylvania Avenue N.W.

★ Dial-a-Park at (202) 619-PARK for a recording of National Park Service events.

★ Dial-a-Museum at (202) 357-2020 (English) or (202) 357-9126 (Spanish) for a 24-hour recorded message of Smithsonian Institution exhibits and activities. TTY (202) 357-1729 for museum information daily between 9:00 am and 4:00 pm.

As you're deciding how to plan your time, it may be helpful to study the centerfold map. A stop at the Observation Deck in the Tower at the Old Post Office is also a good way to get an overview of the monument area. The Tower is located on Pennsylvania Avenue at 12th Street.

One further note — most of the attractions are closed Christmas Day. If you are visiting on other holidays, you might call first to check the hours.

# CHAPTER 1–WELCOME TO WASHINGTON

## HOW TO GET AROUND

**G**etting around can often be confusing in a city that you don't know. Here are some tips to help:

### Metro

The modern efficient Washington subway is a great way to get to many of the sights you'll want to visit. To help you get around, the nearest Metro stop is indicated by the symbol **M** when the subway is within walking distance from the sight. You can also look at the centerfold map which has the Metro stations and the major sights noted. A map of the entire Metro system is on the inside back cover.

When you enter a Metro station, you will need a farecard to pass through the turnstile to the trains. You can get a farecard by putting money in any of the farecard machines. The machine will make change for you. For exact fare information,

## QUICK QUIZ

When you visit the monuments, museums, and memorials of Washington, you'll not only have fun, but you'll also learn a lot. If you want to see that for yourself, take this quiz now. At the end of your visit, take it again. See how much you've learned. The answers are on page 62.

1. Who lives at 1600 Pennsylvania Avenue?
   _____
2. How high is the Washington Monument?
   _____
3. What is the name of the river that divides Washington, D.C. and Virginia?
   _____
4. Name the only president who never lived in the White House.
   _____
5. What is the name of the oldest town in the Washington area?
   _____
6. What other subway runs in Washington besides the Metro?
   _____

7. Who designed the capital city?
   _____
8. Name the only president who was also an architect?
   _____
9. Where is paper money printed?
   _____
10. What are the two parts (or "houses") of Congress called?
    _____
11. Where was Abraham Lincoln assassinated?
    _____
12. Who was Georgetown named after?
    _____
13. What did Japan give to the U.S. that you can see every spring in Washington?
    _____
14. How long a term of office do Supreme Court justices serve?
    _____
15. Where can you see the original Declaration of Independence and the Bill of Rights?
    _____

## CHAPTER 1–WELCOME TO WASHINGTON

which varies by trip length and whether or not it is rush hour, check the signs posted nearby. They will also provide route information for the various lines — red, blue, yellow, orange and green.

### Local Buses

This is the least expensive way to get around the city. You should begin by getting a map of the bus routes from: Washington Metropolitan Area Transit Authority (WMATA), 600 5th Street, N.W.

If you want to call for specific bus route information, dial (202) 637-7000.

Exact fare is required and drivers will not make change. Free transfers to other bus routes are provided depending on where you're going, so you should check with the driver when you get on.

### Taxis

Taxis are the easiest, quickest, and usually most expensive way to get somewhere. Taxis can be called from your hotel or motel, or you can hail one as it passes by.

## METRO MADNESS

1. If you lived in Silver Spring, MD, where would you change for the Blue Line to National Airport?
2. Which Metro lines are primarily east-west routes?
3. If you go on the train in Vienna, VA and get off at Rhode Island Ave., how many stations will you have stopped at altogether?
4. If you want to go from Metro Center to Landover, MD, how many times do you have to change trains?
5. How many stations are there where you can change from one line to another?

Answers on page 62

## StreetSmart

In D.C., the numbered streets run north and south, with the lowest number closest to the Capitol. The streets running east and west of the Capitol are arranged in alphabetical order. Because there are more streets than letters, the alphabet is repeated four times, beginning with the actual letters of the alphabet. The next 26 streets have two-syllable names and are followed by streets with three-syllable names. The fourth alphabet includes streets named for trees and flowers. (By the way, there are numerous exceptions!)

### Sightseeing Tours

An easy way to get around is to make arrangements with companies who run bus tours. You can get schedules in advance that tell the times and places the tours visit and how much they will cost. Check the Yellow Pages of the telephone book under "Sightseeing" for the names of tour companies.

### Tourmobile

An excellent way to see Capitol Hill, the Mall area, and Arlington Cemetery is to take the Tourmobile. You can get on and off at the different stops as often as you want. (The stops are shown on the centerfold map.) Tickets for the Tourmobile can be purchased at the Visitors Center at Arlington Cemetery, at many Mall locations, or when you get on at any of the stops. You can also purchase combination tour tickets to visit Mount Vernon or the Frederick Douglass Home. For more information call (202) 554-7950.

**CHAPTER 2**

# HOW THE CAPITAL WAS BORN

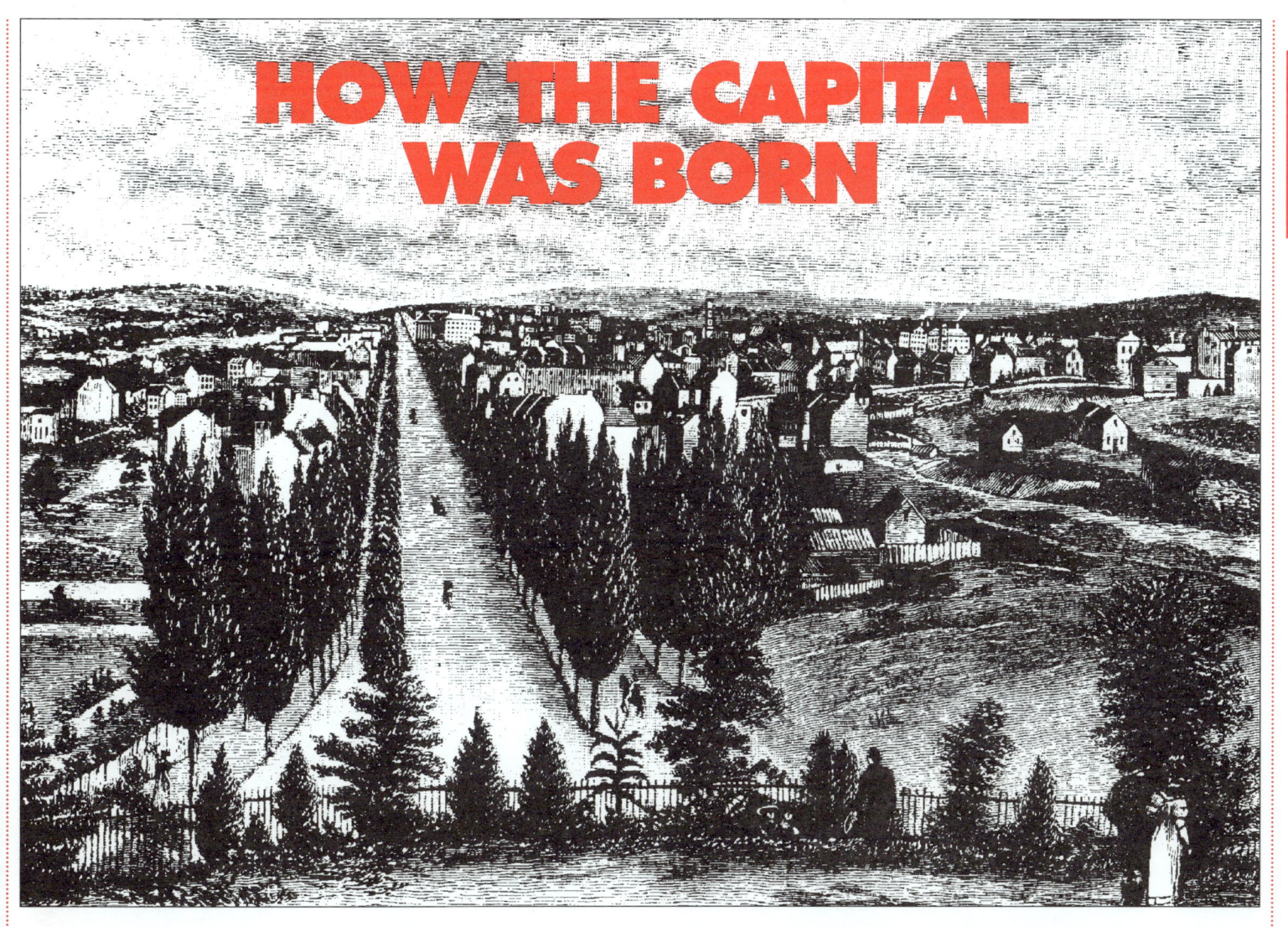

The Revolutionary War was over and the thirteen British colonies were free. The United States of America was a new independent nation. It chose its war hero, General George Washington, to be its first president. Although he hated to leave his home at Mount Vernon, Virginia, Washington proudly went to New York in 1789 to be inaugurated and to begin the enormous task of leading the country.

One of the first problems which the new Congress had to solve was where to put the permanent home of the national government.

Philadelphia was serving as the capital temporarily. Meetings of Congress had also been held in New York City, Baltimore, Annapolis, Trenton, and York. Many cities now wanted the honor of being the capital of the country. There were already squabbles between the North and the South, so the placement of the capital was a very sensitive issue.

It was decided that a new city would be built for the seat of the government, but there was still the question of where it should be. Thomas Jefferson, the new secretary of state, was from

## CHAPTER 2—HOW THE CAPITAL WAS BORN

Virginia and wanted the capital to be near his home. Both he and George Washington thought that the banks of the Potomac River would be the best choice. The Northern leaders were against this location because the Potomac River was in the South. How could this problem be solved?

Alexander Hamilton, the secretary of the treasury, was very interested in getting Congress to pay the Revolutionary War debts. (Wars are expensive to wage — both in terms of human suffering AND money.) You might think this would have nothing to do with choosing a location for the capital. But, surprisingly, it did! Jefferson and Hamilton made a deal. Jefferson would use his influence to get Congress to vote for paying the war debts if Hamilton would persuade the lawmakers to agree on the Potomac River area as the site of the new capital.

Jefferson and Hamilton were successful and the location was finally determined. It would be on the Potomac River near the busy ports of Georgetown and Alexandria.

### L'ENFANT COMES TO WASHINGTON

During the Revolutionary War, the son of a famous French artist came to America to fight in the Revolutionary army. He impressed General Washington with the sketches he drew to keep busy during the bitter winter at Valley Forge. The Frenchman, who rose to the rank of major, was Pierre Charles L'Enfant (pronounced Lonfont). Years after the Valley Forge sketches, he wrote a letter to President Washington expressing his enthusiasm and interest in designing the new capital. L'Enfant was hired. In 1791 he arrived at the shores of the Potomac to begin planning the new city.

Congress had authorized President Washington to buy an area ten miles square, and L'Enfant set out on horseback to study the land that had been chosen. He made note of the ridges and high points and where the land was low and sloping. When it came time to select locations for public buildings, he picked the high points for the major ones so that they could be seen from all over the city. He selected a place called Jenkin's Hill for the Capitol building and wanted a broad avenue to connect it with another spot for the President's Palace (later called the White House). The wide avenue was to be used for parades and marches. (Do you recall watching newly inaugurated presidents pass down Pennsylvania Avenue on TV?)

L'Enfant also picked a site for a monument to George Washington that would form a triangle with these other two important buildings. Between the monument and the Capitol, he pictured fine homes for ambassadors who would be sent to represent foreign countries. Although the area did not become the residences of foreign dignitaries, it is known today as the Mall and is one of the memorable landmarks of our nation's capital.

In other sections of town, L'Enfant's design called for wide streets and many circles. He also divided the city into four sections at the point where the Mall meets the Capitol building. These

*Do you think anyone could throw a silver dollar across the Potomac River?*

## CHAPTER 2—HOW THE CAPITAL WAS BORN

sections are Northeast, Northwest, Southeast, and Southwest. This nomenclature (that means a system of naming) will help you get around the city. In fact, when you write to someone in Washington, every street address is followed by either an N.E., N.W., S.E., or S.W.

In the 1870s, many people thought L'Enfant was crazy to think such a city could ever really be built. It was one of the most ambitious attempts to design a capital that the world had ever seen. People looked and only saw muddy paths, Indian trails, and acres of forest. They doubted the plan would ever work.

L'Enfant was determined to have his plan become a reality, but he often ran into trouble. He did not get along well with the committee assigned to supervise his work. He also angered many people by his decision to tear down the brand new home of a wealthy family because it did not fit in with his plan. The committee urged President Washington to discharge L'Enfant. But the president disagreed and felt it was important for L'Enfant to stay on while the work was still unfinished. L'Enfant continued to do things as he pleased and even asked that members of the committee be replaced. President Washington agreed that THAT was the last straw. L'Enfant had to be dismissed.

After that, L'Enfant only met with hardship. He spent the rest of his life tending a garden in Maryland.

### THE CAPITAL BECOMES A CITY

The remaining work on the city was done by Andrew Ellicott and Benjamin Banneker. They were asked to lay out the streets and decide where the parks should be. Support for the project was needed and money had to be raised. Then came the job of finding people to design and construct the buildings.

When Congress came to the capital city in 1800, it was hardly the city that you see today.

---

### Women OF THE REVOLUTION

While historians debate whether **Betsy Ross** actually sewed the first American flag, it is generally agreed that it was her idea to make the flag.

**Molly Pitcher's** real name was Molly Hays. She got her nickname because she kept bringing pitchers of water to the thirsty soldiers at the Battle of Monmouth. But she was not only a water-woman. When her husband was wounded during the battle, she took over the cannon and fired it herself.

**"Old Mom" Rinker** of Philadelphia sent reports on the British to General Washington in a most unusual fashion. She hid the messages in balls of yarn which she would drop over a cliff.

**Lydia Darrah** kept an eye on British headquarters in Philadelphia for General Washington. She sewed important information into her son's jacket buttons which he wore when he visited the general.

---

The leaders who moved from Philadelphia felt like they were coming to the wilderness. Most of the comforts they had been used to in other cities were nowhere to be found in the new capital.

The city gradually developed and was shaped by the historical events that took place here and by the people who made it their home. As you visit the memorials, monuments, and museums of Washington, you will be able to see the history of our country come to life before your eyes.

**CHAPTER 2–HOW THE CAPITAL WAS BORN**

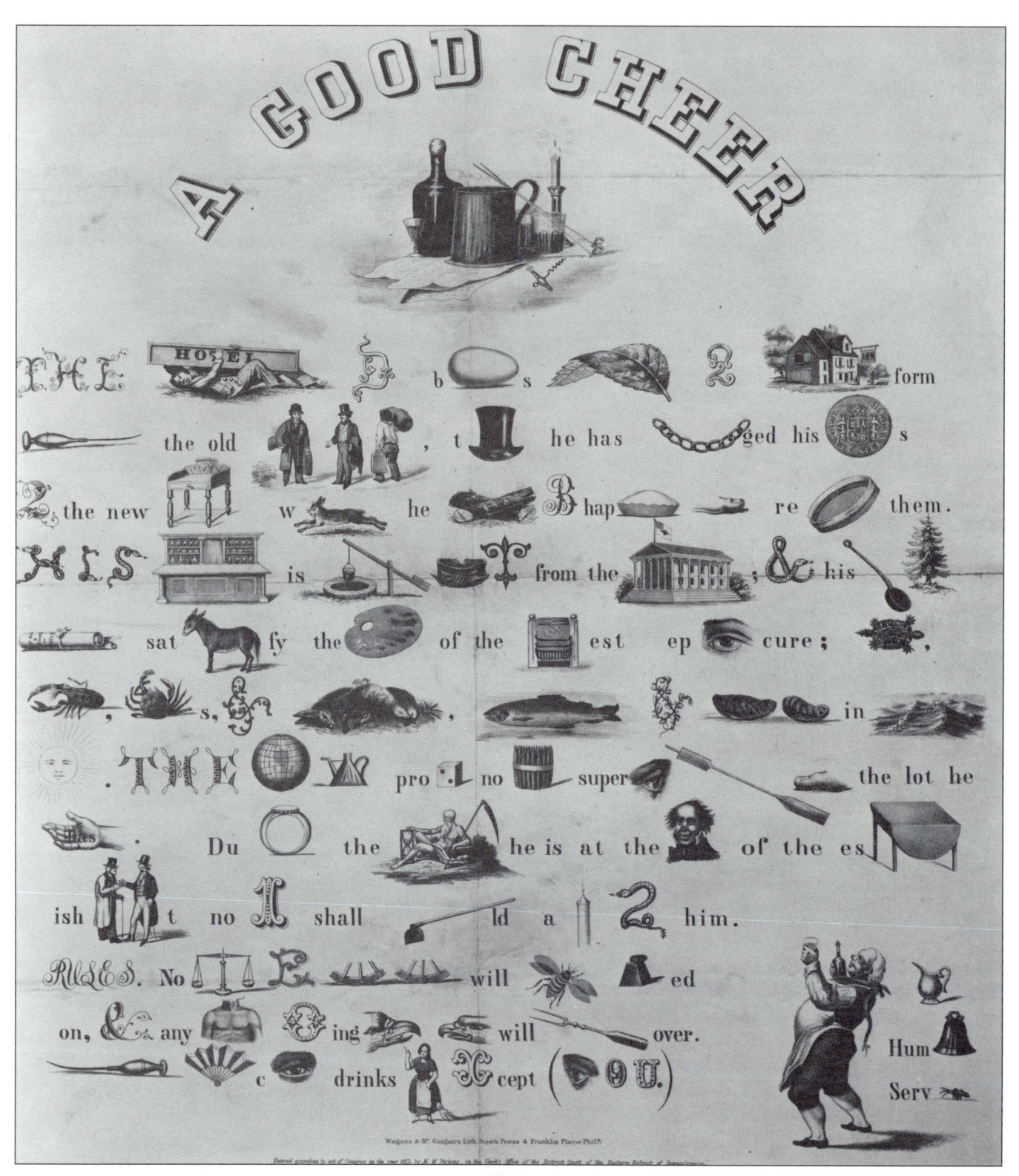

*Early American picture story*

**CHAPTER 3**

# OUR WORKING GOVERNMENT

Some of the most interesting places you'll want to see are those that will give you a better idea of how our government works. While not all of the federal government's activities take place in Washington, they certainly are centered here.

The buildings that represent the three branches of government — the White House (executive branch), the Capitol (legislative branch), and the Supreme Court (judicial branch) — are among the city's most important. Of all the federal government agencies and departments, you'll probably want to add the Bureau of Engraving and Printing and the F.B.I. to your list of "must sees."

Each of these sights welcomes visitors with specially-designed programs. In fact, a tour is the only way you can get in to see the White House, the F.B.I., and the Bureau of Engraving and Printing! There are no guided tours of the Supreme Court, but you will be able to go inside the courtroom if the Court is not in session. The Capitol tour is optional; you are allowed to walk around the building on your own.

As with all the tours around town, one of the best parts is that you'll not only pick up lots of interesting information, but you'll also get a chance to have your questions answered.

## CHAPTER 3–OUR WORKING GOVERNMENT

### BUREAU OF ENGRAVING AND PRINTING
14th and C Streets S.W.
(202) 622-2000
Monday through Friday 9:00 am to 2:00 pm
**M** Smithsonian

**D**id you know that up until a few years ago, every dollar bill ever seen (or spent) started out here at the Bureau of Engraving and Printing? Partly because of the costs of shipping "new" money to banks around the country, in 1991 it was decided to also print money in a location closer to the western states. That is why paper currency is now also printed in Fort Worth, Texas.

The government has been printing all paper money since 1863 and all postage stamps since 1894. Before then private companies printed money and stamps.

You can tour the Bureau in about thirty minutes, and while you watch the entire moneymaking operation — printing, sorting, inspecting, and binding — a recording will describe each step.

Besides money and stamps, there are also hundreds of items printed here such as passports and citizenship documents.

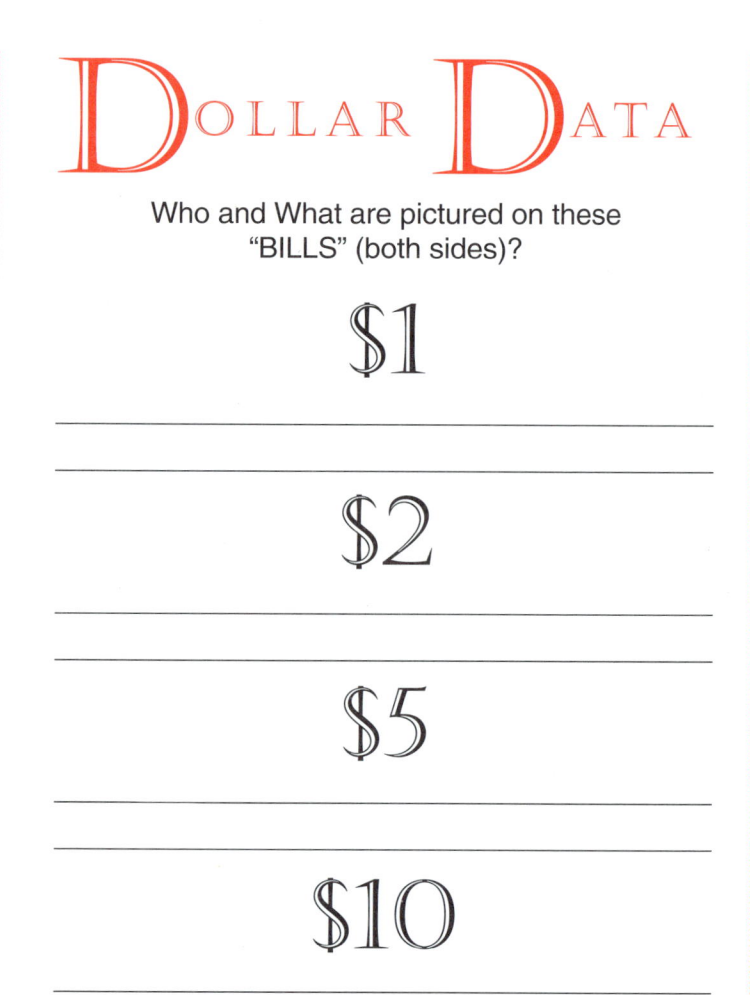

## Dollar Data

Who and What are pictured on these "BILLS" (both sides)?

$1
_____
_____

$2
_____
_____

$5
_____
_____

$10
_____
_____

**Answers on page 62**

## Coin Crazy

When these coins are Heads Up, what presidents do you recognize? How much is this puzzle worth?

**Answers on page 62**

## CHAPTER 3—OUR WORKING GOVERNMENT

# Give a Cheer!

"Two bits, four bits, six bits a dollar" comes from the Spanish dollar that had found its way to the American colonies. It had the number 8 on it. To make change, the piece was cut into smaller parts or "bits."

### DID YOU KNOW?

★ More than 30 million bills are printed here every day.

★ There are no coins here. They are produced in Denver and Philadelphia by the Bureau of the Mint.

★ The $2.00 bill was last printed on Thomas Jefferson's birthday — April 13, 1976.

★ If you tear a $1 bill in half it is worth 50 cents. That is because a bank will replace half the face value of currency IF you have between 2/5 and 3/5 of the original bill. If you have more than 3/5 of the bill, the full value will be given; if you have less than 2/5, you get nothing.

## CAPITOL
Capitol Hill
(202) 224-3121
Daily 9:00 am to 4:30 pm
*Continuous tours until 3:45 lasting 45 minutes*
M Capitol South

The Capitol is the home of Congress. This is where senators and congressmen meet to make the laws for the nation. When the city of Washington was first being planned, the committee in charge faced a major problem. How could they find the best architect to design this important building? They decided to have a contest and offer a prize of $500 for the best entry. The winner was a man from the West Indies, William Thornton — a physician, painter, and inventor. Although based on Thornton's idea, the Capitol that stands today has been greatly enlarged.

On a September morning in 1793, more than 1,500 people came from all over to meet at the President's Park (now called Lafayette Park) and parade to the top of Jenkin's Hill. They watched as President Washington laid the cornerstone of the Senate wing.

*President Washington laying the cornerstone of the Capitol*

## CHAPTER 3 – OUR WORKING GOVERNMENT

*The unfinished Capitol in 1800*

Seven years later when the members of Congress arrived, the only finished part of the Capitol was the Senate. The House of Representatives, the Senate, the Supreme Court, and the Library of Congress all crowded into the newly completed section.

Soon after the House wing was finished, the War of 1812 broke out with the British. President James Madison and his cabinet had been warned that the city of Washington might be attacked. They did not listen and felt that such a terrible thing could never happen. They were wrong and the attack came in the summer of 1814. The Capitol was burned by the British troops.

Then came the task of rebuilding. A copper-covered dome was added and later replaced with a cast-iron dome. The new dome was finished on December 2, 1863 and topped with a bronze Statue of Freedom. The task of building the Capitol was finally over.

When you visit the Capitol and walk around the halls, you'll very likely see some congressmen and senators at work. If they are meeting, you will be able to watch the debates and votes from special seats provided for visitors. If you want to watch Congress at work, you will first have to go to the office of your senator or congressman to get a special pass. While there, sign the guest book and be sure to shake his or her hand and introduce yourself.

### AT THE CAPITOL

You may have noticed that the Capitol has two fronts, one facing the Mall and the other opening onto a large plaza. People from all over the country come to these wide steps to speak their minds. They express their views, no matter how unpopular. This is a right that few countries in the world allow — freedom of speech. From the solitary citizen to the hundreds of thousands who come to demonstrate, this has historically been the place where people come to tell their lawmakers how they feel about issues that are important to them.

Once inside the building you'll enter into a very large room called the rotunda. Look up and see the center of the dome which is richly covered with a painting. The work was done while the artist lay on his back on a platform more than 150 feet up in the air.

Also notice the large paintings around the inside of the rotunda. They illustrate important historical events such as the signing of the Declaration of Independence and the landing of Christopher Columbus.

Then walk into Statuary Hall. Before additions

### Capital & Capitol

**Capital** - a city that is the seat of government of a state or nation. (There are several other meanings you can find in the dictionary.)

**Capitol** - the building in which the U.S. Congress meets in Washington, D.C. (or the building in which a state legislature meets).

# CHAPTER 3–OUR WORKING GOVERNMENT

were made to the building in 1857, this room was used for the meetings of the House of Representatives. The statues here were given by each state to honor famous people. See if you can find the statues from your state.

In the chamber where the House of Representatives meets today, see the 435 seats arranged in a semicircle with an aisle running down the middle. The Democrats sit on the left side, the Republicans on the right.

If you get to watch a session going on, you can see that when certain votes are taken, the representatives insert a card into a little box near their seats. The results of the vote are automatically flashed on a big board for all to see. When other votes are taken, the representatives call out their "yeas" and "nays."

The Senate chamber looks very different from the chamber of the House of Representatives. The room is smaller and there are desks arranged in a semicircle by seniority — according to who has been a senator the longest. There are some exceptions such as Senator Ted Kennedy who uses his brother John's desk.

## DID YOU KNOW?

★ You can always tell which house of Congress is meeting because an American flag is raised over that wing. At night if there are sessions going on, the top part of the dome will be lit.

★ During the Civil War, President Abraham Lincoln was often criticized for continuing the construction of the Capitol. There were those who felt the War needed all the funds and manpower. Lincoln said, "If the people see the Capitol going on, it is a sign we intend the Union shall go on."

★ George Washington was supposed to be buried below the rotunda, but his relatives wanted his grave to remain at his home at Mount Vernon.

★ During the Civil War, the Capitol was used as a hospital, and there was a bakery in the basement where thousands of loaves of bread were baked daily.

*The United States Capitol*

## CHAPTER 3—OUR WORKING GOVERNMENT

The senators and representatives meet in the Capitol, but their offices and staff are in other buildings nearby. To make the senators' trip to the Capitol easier and quicker, an underground train was built to connect the Senate offices to the Capitol. You can take a ride on this subway and visit the Russell, Dirksen, and Hart Office Buildings.

The representatives do not have a special subway, but an underground passageway connects their offices with the Capitol. These offices are in the Cannon, Longworth, and Rayburn Office Buildings.

## Joking Around

"What do you call a spy in bed?"
"An undercover agent!"

"Knock, knock"
"Who's there?"
"A visitor who can't find the doorbell!"

### FEDERAL BUREAU OF INVESTIGATION (F.B.I.)

J. Edgar Hoover Building
10th Street and Pennsylvania Avenue N.W.
(202) 324-3447
Monday through Friday 8:45 am to 4:15 pm
*Tours every 15 minutes lasting 1 hour*
[M] Archives-Navy Memorial

Is there anyone who hasn't heard of the F.B.I.? Well, now you'll get a chance to see just how the super agents track down their suspects. The F.B.I. not only tries to catch bank robbers, but also keeps a check on people it feels are dangerous to our government.

The work of tracking down suspected criminals means looking at all possible clues — blood stains on a handkerchief, bullets that have been fired, and fingerprints on a telephone where the crime occurred. You'll be able to see how the F.B.I. does

### DID YOU KNOW?

★ Fingerprints are a foolproof way to identify someone. It's because no two people in the whole world have the same ones — not even identical twins.

★ The F.B.I. has more than 207,000,000 fingerprints on file.

★ There are three basic types of fingerprints:
1. Loops - the lines all bend in a loop.
2. Whorls - a circle in the center surrounded by other circles.
3. Arches - an arch form in the center and surrounding lines curving around it.

*Loops*   *Whorls*   *Arches*

## CHAPTER 3—OUR WORKING GOVERNMENT

its work, and even get to watch an expert give a shooting demonstration. But no need to worry, his target is made of paper.

The way to see the F.B.I. is to take a tour around the building. You'll learn all about many of the famous cases that the agents have cracked and see pictures of the "Ten Most Wanted Criminals." You'll also find out that many criminals are caught thanks to "tips" from ordinary citizens.

### CODE INFO

Codes and ciphers are ways to write a message so that only someone with a "key" is able to read it. Cryptography (the art of making codes) dates back to ancient Greeks. In fact, the word cryptography is based on the Greek words for "hidden" and "writing."

Throughout history people have used codes to keep their messages secret. Julius Caesar used a code in which each letter was replaced by a letter three places to its right in the normal alphabet. For example, using our alphabet, "My fellow Romans" (from a famous speech in Shakespeare's play *Julius Caesar*) would be "Pb Ihoorz Urpdqv." Try writing your name in Caesar's code.

### FIND THE CLUES

#### WHO AM I?

1. I am always remembered for my honesty. During the Civil War, I tried to keep the Union together. *Who am I?*

2. I am known for my nightly displays of concerts, operas, and plays. *Who am I?*

3. Sometimes you can look in me and see the reflection of the Washington Monument. *Who am I?*

4. I am a monument to the unknown soldiers who have died for our country. *Who am I?*

5. I am a storehouse of books, films, and photographs. Every book here has my name written inside. *Who am I?*

6. I am a museum which tells the story of the African people. *Who am I?*

7. The C & O Canal was supposed to reach me, but it never did. *Who am I?*

8. I used to be called the President's Palace. *Who am I?*

**Answers on page 62**

## Crack That Code

These are called box ciphers. Can you decipher the messages?

**Answers on page 62**

1.  T O Y T S I
    O U U A L R
    B H G H O U
    E A V E T O
    A G O O D T

2.  Y E H E T
    D K T R N
    L I E P E
    U L B S D
    O U O U I
    W O T E S

# CHAPTER 3—OUR WORKING GOVERNMENT

## SUPREME COURT

First and East Capitol Streets N.E.
(202) 479-3000
Monday through Friday 9:00 am to 4:30 pm
*15-minute "talk" every half hour (when Court is NOT in session)*
[M] Capitol South

The United States Supreme Court is the highest court of the land, but it has its roots in every town in the nation. Did you ever go into the courtroom in your local courthouse? A case starting there could finally be decided years later in this majestic building.

While all courts have the responsibility for interpreting our laws, the Supreme Court has the final say on many of the important issues which affect all the people in the country. The Supreme Court is even more powerful than Congress, as it can decide that a law passed by Congress violates the Constitution and is not legal.

*The United States Supreme Court*

### DID YOU KNOW?

★ There have only been 16 chief justices in the Court's history.

★ No woman served on the Court until 1981 when Sandra Day O'Connor was appointed.

*Inside the Supreme Court in 1888*

## EQUAL JUSTICE UNDER LAW
*(carved on west side of Supreme Court Building)*
What does this mean to you?

There are eight associate justices and a chief justice who are appointed by the president to serve on the Court for the rest of their lives. Why do you think the Founding Fathers felt a lifetime term was important?

When you see the white marble building, you can't help but be impressed. Climb the stairs and enter into the red velvet courtroom. Can you feel that the decisions made here must be very, very important ones? The Court is in session only part of the year (October to June), but whether or not you get to see the Court in action, it is still an interesting place to visit.

# CHAPTER 3 – OUR WORKING GOVERNMENT

## Curious Court Customs

- At the start of each day, a new quill pen is placed before each attorney arguing a case.
- The chief justice sits in the center with associate justices seated in order of who has been on the Court the longest. The justices at the ends of the table are those that are newest to the Court.
- "Oyez, Oyez, Oyez"...that is the voice of the Supreme Court crier announcing that the Supreme Court is in session.
- The Supreme Court has its own independent police force whose jurisdiction (or responsibility) is the Court's single block area.

## TRUE OR FALSE

1. The man who was chosen to design the capital city was Italian.
2. George Washington's doctor lived in Alexandria, Virginia.
3. The Bureau of Engraving and Printing makes bills, stamps, and coins.
4. During the War of 1812, the painting of George Washington in the White House was burned.
5. The senators have a special subway to get from their office buildings to the Capitol.
6. Georgetown was a city before Washington, D.C. was built.

**Answers on page 62**

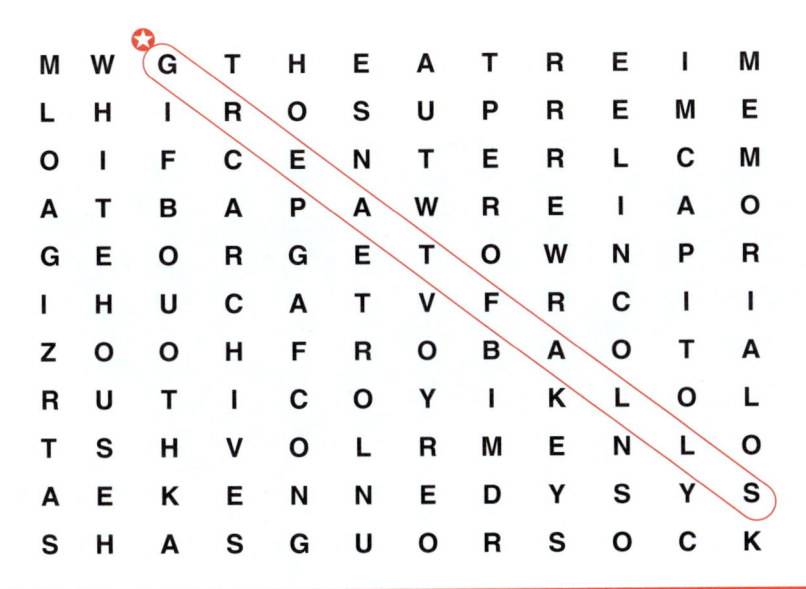

## WASHINGTON SEARCH

```
M W G T H E A T R E I M
L H I R O S U P R E M E
O I F C E N T E R L C M
A T B A P A W R E I A O
G E O R G E T O W N P R
I H U C A T V F R C I I
Z O O H F R O B A O T A
R U T I C O Y I K L O L
T S H V O L R M E N L O
A E K E N N E D Y S Y S
S H A S G U O R S O C K
```

Find and circle where these places are hiding in the box on the left.

- ★ GREAT FALLS
- WHITE HOUSE
- GEORGETOWN
- CAPITOL
- FBI
- LINCOLN
- MEMORIAL
- ARCHIVES
- LIBRARY
- KENNEDY
- CENTER
- ZOO
- SUPREME
- FORDS
- THEATRE

**Answers on page 62**

# CHAPTER 3—OUR WORKING GOVERNMENT

## WHITE HOUSE
1600 Pennsylvania Avenue N.W.
(202) 456-1414
Tuesday through Saturday 10:00 am to noon
*Pick up same-day tickets at White House Visitor Center after 8:00 am at Department of Commerce, 1450 Pennsylvania Avenue.*
**M** McPherson Square or Metro Center

When Abigail Adams arrived at the "President's Palace" to join her husband John in November of 1800, she shuddered at the thought of living in what appeared to be a mass of rubble. Construction had begun years earlier but, as with the rest of the city of Washington, plans were delayed, changed, and generally confused. So Abigail Adams was forced to use the East Room to dry the family laundry. It was hardly a presidential palace in 1800. Gradually, work on the house was finished, and it became a suitable place for a president and his family to live.

Then, on August 24, 1814, a terrible disaster occurred. British troops captured the city. President Madison was on the battlefront and saw that it was a losing fight. He sent a note to his wife, Dolley, urging her to pick up and leave. Time was short and the troops were nearby. Leaving many personal belongings behind, she hurried to have the oil painting of George Washington cut out of its frame and taken with her for safekeeping. It was good thinking. The President's Palace was burned, leaving little more than the outside shell.

Building began again in 1815, and two years later it was ready for the First Family. Each president and family since John Adams has added its own personality and style to that famous place you know so well as the White House.

As you would expect, the home of the presidents has gone through continuous changes and improvements throughout its history. In 1834, running water took the place of waterwells, and in 1848, gaslights replaced oil lamps. In those years, these things were considered as luxurious as private movie theaters and swimming pools are today.

*The White House*

## CHAPTER 3—OUR WORKING GOVERNMENT

In 1948, it was found that all of the alterations had made the building so weak as to be dangerous. President Harry Truman moved out of the White House into the Blair House across the street, and a complete restoration was begun. The original atmosphere of the house was carefully preserved while making the structure stronger and more livable.

In keeping with the historic atmosphere of the building, President Kennedy's wife Jacqueline began a program of decorating and furnishing the rooms in authentic early 19th century style. In that way, the inside of the White House would "fit" the outside.

When you walk through the different rooms of the White House, you will see portraits of the presidents and First Ladies, antiques, and gifts from all over the world. Imagine the exciting events that have taken place here...the balls and receptions in the East Room, the dinners for royal visitors in the State Dining Room. Remember that you are in much more than a museum of American history. You are also in the building where the president has his offices. This is where he meets with the most important and powerful people in the world to make decisions which can change history. AND you are in the place where presidents and their families eat, sleep, watch TV, and do all of the other things that you and your family do in your own home.

*The Oval Office*

### WHO PROTECTS THE PREZ?

Have you ever wondered who all those people are crowded around the president when he is out in public? Chances are they are members of the United States Secret Service. The Secret Service has been providing presidential protection since 1901. Before then, three American presidents had been shot in 36 years. You may recall that Abraham Lincoln was assassinated, but you may not know that Presidents Garfield and McKinley were also gunshot victims.

Today the Secret Service also protects the president's family; the vice president and his family; former presidents and their families; major candidates for president and vice president and their spouses; visiting heads of foreign governments; and other people the president decides require special protection.

# CHAPTER 3—OUR WORKING GOVERNMENT

## DID YOU KNOW?

★ George Washington was the only president who did not live in the White House.

★ There are 132 rooms in the White House. Of these, 30 make up the president's family living quarters.

★ In 1807 two grizzly bears resided briefly (in cages) on the White House lawn. They were brought back by Lewis and Clark as souvenirs of their Northwest exploration.

★ Grover Cleveland became the first president to wed in the White House. His sweetheart was Frances Folsom.

★ The White House has been called that as early as 1808, but President Roosevelt made it the official name in 1902.

## PRESIDENTIAL TIDBITS

• William Henry Harrison served the shortest time in office…only one month in 1841. Did you know that his grandson Benjamin Harrison became our 23rd president?

• Franklin Roosevelt was the first president to appear on television. Why don't you think presidents before him went on TV?

• While John F. Kennedy was the youngest man ever ELECTED president (at age 43), Theodore Roosevelt was the youngest to ever serve in office. Roosevelt was 42 when he took over the office upon the death of President William McKinley.

• Until the 12th Amendment was passed, the vice president and president did not "run" on the same ticket. Instead, the vice president's job went to the man who got the second highest number of votes in the presidential election. This changed because of the growth and strength of political parties. Do you think it's better that the top two offices be held by people who support each other's views?

## WHAT ABOUT THE PRESIDENT'S CABINET?

You probably already know that the term "cabinet" does not refer to a piece of furniture in the Oval Office. But did you know that it comes from a term used in 18th century England and refers to a private meeting room? James Madison was the first to use the term to describe a president's advisers.

While presidents have had official advisers since the beginning of our country, there is no law requiring that there be any nor that their advice actually be taken. Over the years, the names of different cabinet positions have changed and their numbers have grown.

In George Washington's cabinet, Henry Knox was the secretary of war. Today those duties are handled by a secretary of defense. In Washington's day do you think he had a secretary of energy? Do you think a shrinking ozone layer and endangered species were problems back then?

Did you know that when a cabinet member has finished serving a president, he usually is given his leather chair (with nameplate on the back) to take with him?

# CHAPTER 3—OUR WORKING GOVERNMENT

# Name Game

Draw a line from the name to the matching face.

**Harry S. Truman**

**Abraham Lincoln**

**George Washington**

**Ulysses S. Grant**

**Theodore Roosevelt**

Answers on page 62

## WHAT HAPPENS WHERE?

How well do you know what happens where in Washington? Pick the right place from the list below and fill in the blanks.

1. The military headquarters of the United States are located in the _____.
2. The president's office is called the _____.
3. Congressmen make laws in the _____.
4. White House outdoor events are held in the _____.
5. The area between the Capitol and the Washington Monument is called the _____.

A. Rose Garden    B. Pentagon    C. Mall
D. Capitol    E. Oval Office

Answers on page 62

## NICKNAMES

Kids have nicknames and so do some politicians. Some are flattering and based on accomplishments; others are not.

Can you figure which presidents belong to these?

1. Ike
2. Honest Abe
3. Tippecanoe
4. Napoleon of the Stump
5. Old Rough and Ready
6. F.D.R.

Answers on page 62

23

**CHAPTER 4**

# MONUMENTS AND MEMORIALS
## HONORING OUR HISTORY

You can tell a lot about a country by what it considers important about its history. Our nation's history, like your own family history, is passed on through what we read, what we see, and mostly through what we are told.

Think for a minute. If your parents didn't tell you about your family background, such as where your ancestors came from or how tall or talented they were, you wouldn't really have a history. You'd know you had a past, but you wouldn't know much more. Well, a country's history is a lot like that. One of the ways we recognize important people and events is by building memorials and monuments to them. It is a way of making sure that their stories continue to be told.

As you tour the Lincoln Memorial, the Washington Monument, Arlington Cemetery and the other sights described in this chapter, keep in mind the values and ideals that are embodied in the leaders and institutions that we as a nation have chosen to honor.

*The Washington Monument in 1854*

*Raising money to build the Washington Monument*

# CHAPTER 4 – MONUMENTS AND MEMORIALS

## ARLINGTON NATIONAL CEMETERY
Arlington, Virginia (703) 692-0931
Daily 8:00 am to 7:00 pm
Closes at 5:00 pm October — March
**M** Arlington Cemetery

**W**hen you walk through the cemetery you will see the graves of United States soldiers. From the Civil War to the Vietnam War, this cemetery honors their memory.

Among those buried here are two people you have heard much about — President John F. Kennedy and his brother Senator Robert F. Kennedy. A flame burning all the time stands vigil over the late president's grave. Near the grave, his wife Jacqueline is buried and so are a son and daughter. You can see by the tombstones that the children were infants when they died. Also notice that there are irregular stones over the grave area. These were brought from Cape Cod, Massachusetts, where the late president spent many vacations.

*John F. Kennedy*

As you tour the cemetery, stop and look at the uniformed guard marching with his rifle back and forth in front of the Tomb of the Unknown Soldier. Day and night a guard is posted here, and every hour (or half hour from April through September) you can see the changing of the guard. The Tomb honors those soldiers who have died in battle but whose identities could never be determined. A soldier who died during World War I is buried in the white marble Tomb. In front, notice the three graves honoring unknown soldiers of World War II, and the Korean and Vietnam Wars.

## NAME FAME

**W**e also often honor people by naming buildings, streets, towns, and even people after them. Washington, D.C. has Woodrow Wilson and Calvin Coolidge High Schools. The part of the city known as Georgetown was named after King George II of England. There is Martin Luther King Jr. Avenue and the George Washington Memorial Parkway. The House and Senate office buildings were named for respected leaders in Congress. The list goes on and on.

What examples can you think of from your hometown? Are there "famous name" airports or streets in places you have visited or heard about? Write them in the space below. Ask your parents or teacher if you are not sure why the person was honored.

_____
_____
_____
_____
_____
_____
_____
_____

## CHAPTER 4—MONUMENTS AND MEMORIALS

### KENNEDY CENTER FOR THE PERFORMING ARTS

New Hampshire Avenue at F Street N.W.
(202) 416-8340
Daily 10:00 am to late evening
*Continuous tours between 10:00 am and 1:00 pm lasting 1 hour*
Ⓜ Foggy Bottom

*The Kennedy Center for the Performing Arts*

The white marble Kennedy Center stands on the banks of the Potomac River. The building provides not only excellent theater events but serves as a living memorial to the late President John F. Kennedy.

Enter through the large glass doors — you'll get the red carpet treatment! There are two main entrances. You will either pass under the flags from all over the world that hang in the Hall of Nations, or walk down the Hall of States and see the flags of our country. You will come to another room called the Grand Foyer which leads to three theaters. These are the Eisenhower Theater (named after the late president), the Opera House, and the Concert Hall. A smaller theater, called the Terrace Theater, is on the rooftop level.

The American Film Institute Theater is also located in the Kennedy Center. It is the only theater in the building which does not have "live" entertainment, but there are often lectures and discussions by movie producers, directors, and actors about the films that are being shown.

The entire building is decorated with gifts from many nations. In the Grand Foyer notice the huge bronze head of President Kennedy and walk out to the terrace for a fine view of the Potomac River and Georgetown. An even better view is from the rooftop level, which you can reach by elevator.

### LINCOLN MEMORIAL

West End of Mall (202) 426-6895
Open all the time
Ⓜ Foggy Bottom

Abraham Lincoln, our sixteenth president, is remembered not only for his leadership during the difficult years of the Civil War but also for his personal qualities. You may have heard stories about "Honest Abe," or how he taught himself to read when he was just a boy living in Illinois.

Later, he studied law and became interested in politics. He ran for the Senate in Illinois against Stephen A. Douglas and challenged him to public debates. Although Lincoln lost the election, he had become well-known from the debates, and in 1860, he became the Republican presidential candidate. At that time, the Union was weakened by differences that divided the North and South, especially the issue of slavery. When Lincoln won the election, the South took that as a sign that their problems with the North could not be worked out. One by one they seceded (dropped out) from the Union. The stage was set for the beginning of the Civil War.

By the time the war was over in 1865, more Americans had died than in any other war in the history of the country. And while there was joy that the war was over, there was also sadness at

*The Lincoln Memorial*

## CHAPTER 4—MONUMENTS AND MEMORIALS

*Statue of Abraham Lincoln*

the death of President Abraham Lincoln. He was assassinated five days after Lee surrendered. The nation lost a great leader.

To honor this hero, plans were made to build a large memorial. There were many arguments over what kind of memorial should be built and where it should be.

It was not until 1912 that the current site was chosen by the Congress and Henry Bacon selected to design the building. When the cornerstone was laid on the anniversary of Lincoln's birthday in 1915, two small copper boxes were placed inside. The boxes contain the story of Lincoln's life, a Bible, his autograph, and other important papers.

When you climb the stairs to the memorial, you'll be staring at the huge seated figure of Abraham Lincoln. The statue is nineteen-feet tall and was sculpted by Daniel Chester French. After you've taken all your pictures…stop. Look around you. Try to shut out the noise of the other people. Turn to the left and read the words carved into the wall. They should be familiar to you. It's the Gettysburg Address. Lincoln spoke these words when the cemetery on the Gettysburg Battlefield was dedicated. The mural above the Address shows the Angel of Truth freeing a slave, which is symbolic of Lincoln and the Civil War.

To the right of the statue, notice that parts of Lincoln's Second Inaugural Address are carved into the wall. The mural above shows the Angel of Truth joining the hands of the North and of the South.

As you leave the memorial, look out at the Washington Monument, and if it's a clear sunny day, you will be able to see the column's reflection in the Reflecting Pool.

### TONGUE TWISTERS

Try saying these tongue twisters ten times fast. Can you do it?

- **Long-legged lean Lincoln loathed lies.**
- **Franklin fretted for fellows finding fools for friends.**
- **Stately seated stone statues silently stare.**

### DID YOU KNOW?

★ Lincoln did not grow his beard until after he was elected president. Tradition has it that his whiskers came about at the suggestion of 11-year-old Grace Bedell who wrote to Lincoln shortly before the election. By the time he traveled from Springfield to Washington for the inauguration, his beard was almost fully grown.

★ The Lincoln Memorial was built on land that used to be a swamp.

★ The thirty-six columns surrounding the building stand for the number of states that were in the nation when Lincoln died.

## CHAPTER 4–MONUMENTS AND MEMORIALS

### MARINE CORPS WAR MEMORIAL
(Iwo Jima Statue)
Virginia side of Memorial Bridge between Arlington Cemetery and Arlington Blvd.

**T**his statue was modeled after the most famous news photo of World War II. The photograph was taken after a bloody battle on the Japanese island of Iwo Jima in the Pacific Ocean. Six Marines were carrying the American flag to the top of the highest peak on the island to proclaim their victory.

The memorial is dedicated to all of the Marines who have died in battle. Did you notice that the flag they are holding is real? It flies all the time.

*Iwo Jima Statue*

*The Thomas Jefferson Memorial*

### THOMAS JEFFERSON MEMORIAL
Tidal Basin Drive
East Potomac Park
(202) 426-6821
Open all the time

**T**homas Jefferson was the author of the Declaration of Independence, secretary of state under George Washington, and the third president of the United States. He died in 1826, more than a century before plans were made to build a memorial to him. Jefferson was a man of many talents. The graceful white structure on the southern end of the Tidal Basin is a fitting monument to his memory.

The circular building topped with a low dome reflects Jefferson's long-standing fascination with dome structures. He himself had designed several buildings with domes, including his beautiful

## CHAPTER 4–MONUMENTS AND MEMORIALS

home in Virginia called Monticello. Did you know that Thomas Jefferson was the only president who was also an architect?

When you visit the Jefferson Memorial, look above the entranceway before you go in. Do you recognize any of the figures in the sculpture? These are the men who wrote the Declaration of Independence — Thomas Jefferson, Benjamin Franklin, John Adams, Roger Sherman, and Robert Livingston.

Inside, the nineteen-foot bronze figure of Thomas Jefferson stands wearing a long fur-lined coat, knee pants, and buckled shoes. Rudolph Evans was selected from among many sculptors who entered a contest to win the honor of designing the statue.

The writings on the four walls are a very important part of this memorial. Don't overlook them. On one wall are important lines from the Declaration of Independence, which Jefferson considered to be one of his greatest achievements. On another are his ideas about freedom of the mind. His view on slavery is written on a third wall, and on the fourth are his ideas about government, claiming that "laws and institutions must go hand in hand with the progress of the human mind." Jefferson felt very strongly that the rights and responsibilities of the citizens must be protected, and that the government must not abuse its powers in ways that limit these rights.

The Jefferson Memorial was dedicated on April 13, 1943, the 200th anniversary of Thomas Jefferson's birth. With its flowering cherry blossom trees in springtime, the memorial is certainly one of the city's prettiest sights.

### NAME THAT YEAR

1. The Declaration of Independence was signed in _____.
2. The city of Washington was burned by British troops during the War of _____.
3. The Civil War ended in _____.
4. Georgetown became part of Washington in _____.
5. Abraham Lincoln was assassinated in _____.
6. The cornerstone of the Capitol was laid by George Washington in _____.
7. Congress came to Washington in _____.
8. The Capitol was finished in _____.

*Answers on page 62*

1793   1812
1865   1776

## CHAPTER 4—MONUMENTS AND MEMORIALS

### VIETNAM VETERANS MEMORIAL
West End of Mall
Open all the time
M Foggy Bottom

The Vietnam War happened when your parents were teenagers and young adults— probably just a little older than you are now. It was a war that divided the country with many people feeling we should not be fighting; other people felt it was our duty to fight there. It was our nation's longest war.

The memorial was built on land owned by our government, but the actual structure was built with money given by many, many citizens. The idea of a memorial came from Jan Scruggs, a Vietnam veteran, who wanted to honor the more than 58,000 Americans who gave their lives or who were missing in action.

A contest was held to pick the best design for a monument. A 21-year-old Yale University student named Maya Ying Lin of Athens, Ohio had the winning entry. "The names would become the memorial," Lin said.

Visitors take rubbings on paper of the names of loved ones that are inscribed forever on the memorial's black granite walls. Some leave flowers and other remembrances. The hushed setting includes a life-size sculpture of America's fighting men in action forever facing the names on the Wall.

Nearby you will see the **VIETNAM WOMEN'S MEMORIAL** which honors the more than 265,000 military women who served in Vietnam. This sculpture portrays three Vietnam-era women and shows one of them caring for a wounded male soldier. Like the Wall, the memorial was paid for by contributions from individual citizens around the country. Many of these people felt that the efforts of women soldiers had been forgotten.

*The Vietnam Veterans Memorial*

**CHAPTER 4—MONUMENTS AND MEMORIALS**

## WASHINGTON MONUMENT
Center of the Mall
Constitution Avenue at 15th Street N.W.
(202) 426-6839
Daily 8:00 am to midnight Spring/Summer
9:00 am to 5:00 pm Labor Day — Mar. 31
M Smithsonian

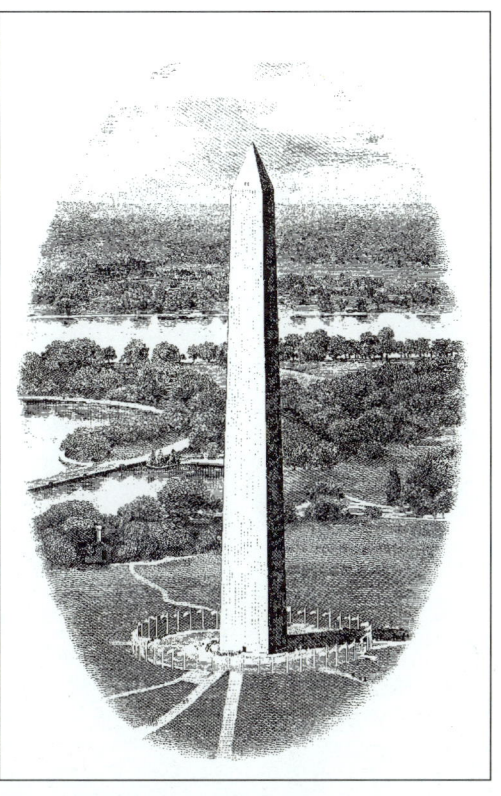

The Washington Monument is probably the most familiar landmark in the capital. It stands 555 feet 5 1/8 inches high and wears its marble proudly. You can see that there are no windows until the very top, which you can reach by elevator. The view is spectacular from here.

*The Washington Monument*

The idea of building a monument to George Washington was first thought of in 1783. At that time, the leaders of the new country thought a statue of Washington on his horse would be a fitting tribute to the Revolutionary War hero. President Washington even approved the spot that L'Enfant had picked for the monument to him. But it was not until after his death that a monument was actually built.

Although Congress had plans to honor Washington, it was a new organization, the Washington National Monument Society, that was formed to raise money for the project. A contest was held and the obelisk that now stands is based on the winning design. The obelisk form

## Name that Noodle

One word is wrong in each of these famous quotations. Every time you see NOODLE or NOODLES write in the correct word from the NOODLE NOOK.

**1.** These are the times that try men's NOODLES."
_____

**2.** "Give me liberty or give me NOODLES."
_____

**3.** "Don't give up the NOODLE."
_____

**4.** "Speak softly and carry a big NOODLE."
_____

**5.** "Don't fire until you see the whites of their NOODLES." _____

**6.** "I have not yet begun to NOODLE."
_____

**7.** "...government of the NOODLE, by the NOODLE, and for the NOODLE." _____

**8.** "The only NOODLE we have to fear is fear itself."
_____

**9.** "We hold these NOODLES to be self-evident that all men are created equal." _____

**10.** "Ask not what your NOODLE can do for you, but what you can do for your NOODLE."
_____

### Noodle Nook
thing   truths   fight
ship   souls   people
country   stick   death   eyes

*Answers on page 62*

31

32

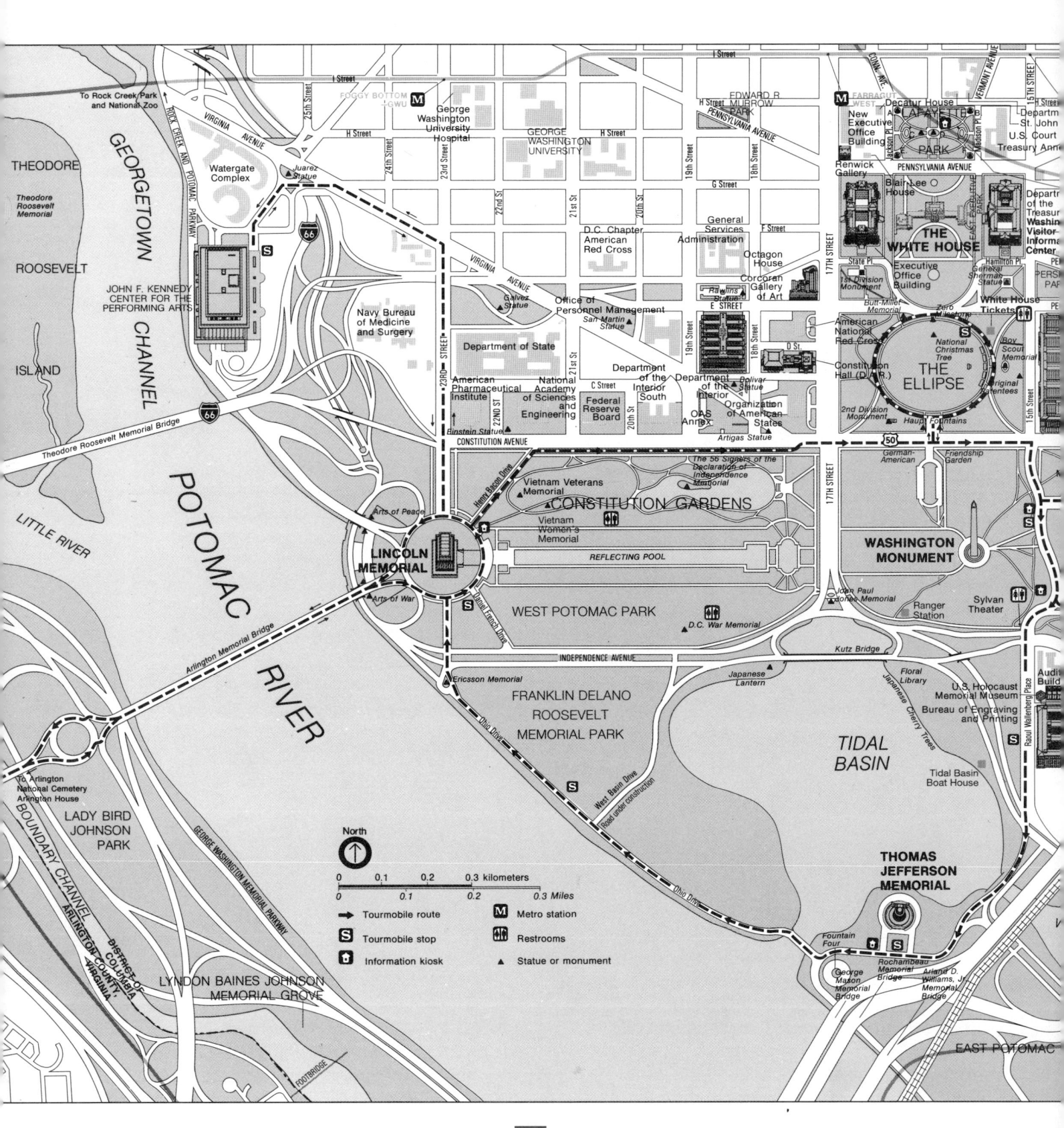

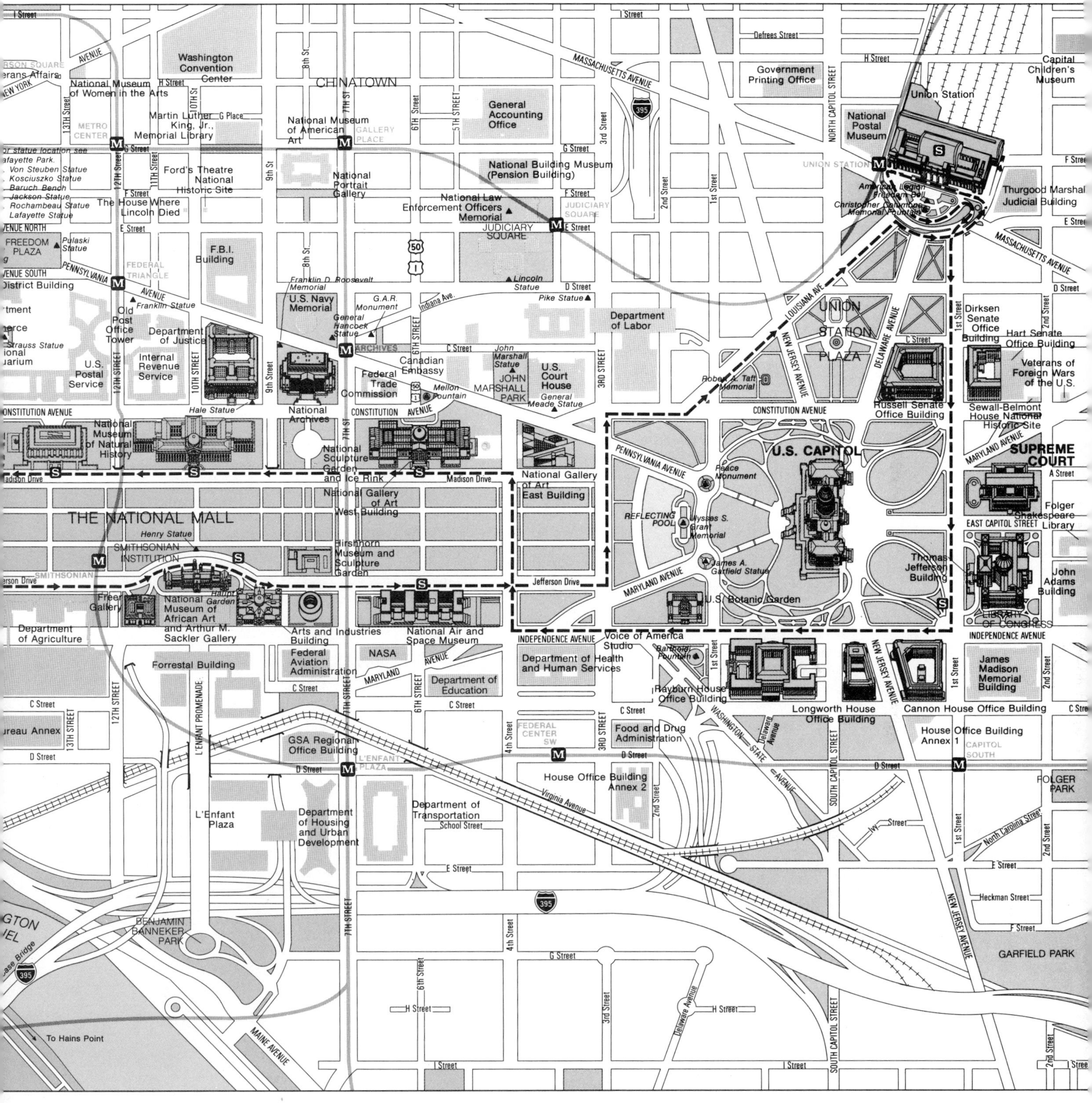

Washington Convention Center
CHINATOWN
National Museum of Women in the Arts
Martin Luther King, Jr., Memorial Library
National Museum of American Art
National Portrait Gallery
Ford's Theatre National Historic Site
The House Where Lincoln Died
Government Printing Office
General Accounting Office
National Building Museum (Pension Building)
National Law Enforcement Officers Memorial
JUDICIARY SQUARE
Union Station
National Postal Museum
Capital Children's Museum
Thurgood Marshal Judicial Building
F.B.I. Building
FEDERAL TRIANGLE
District Building
Old Post Office Tower
Department of Justice
Internal Revenue Service
U.S. Postal Service
U.S. Navy Memorial
Franklin D. Roosevelt Memorial
G.A.R. Monument
General Hancock Statue
ARCHIVES
Canadian Embassy
Federal Trade Commission
Mellon Fountain
John Marshall Statue
JOHN MARSHALL PARK
U.S. Court House
General Meade Statue
Department of Labor
Lincoln Statue
Pike Statue
UNION STATION PLAZA
Robert A. Taft Memorial
Dirksen Senate Office Building
Hart Senate Office Building
Veterans of Foreign Wars of the U.S.
Russell Senate Office Building
Sewall-Belmont House National Historic Site
SUPREME COURT
Folger Shakespeare Library
National Museum of Natural History
National Archives
National Sculpture Garden and Ice Rink
National Gallery of Art West Building
National Gallery of Art East Building
THE NATIONAL MALL
Henry Statue
SMITHSONIAN INSTITUTION
Hirshhorn Museum and Sculpture Garden
U.S. CAPITOL
Peace Monument
REFLECTING POOL
Ulysses S. Grant Memorial
James A. Garfield Statue
U.S. Botanic Garden
Thomas Jefferson Building
John Adams Building
LIBRARY OF CONGRESS
Freer Gallery
National Museum of African Art and Arthur M. Sackler Gallery
Arts and Industries Building
National Air and Space Museum
Department of Agriculture
Forrestal Building
Federal Aviation Administration
NASA
Department of Education
Voice of America Studio
Department of Health and Human Services
Bartholdi Fountain
Rayburn House Office Building
Longworth House Office Building
Cannon House Office Building
James Madison Memorial Building
Food and Drug Administration
House Office Building Annex 1
House Office Building Annex 2
GSA Regional Office Building
L'Enfant Plaza
Department of Housing and Urban Development
Department of Transportation
FEDERAL CENTER SW
CAPITOL SOUTH
FOLGER PARK
GARFIELD PARK
BENJAMIN BANNEKER PARK
To Hains Point
PENNSYLVANIA AVENUE
CONSTITUTION AVENUE
INDEPENDENCE AVENUE
MASSACHUSETTS AVENUE
NEW JERSEY AVENUE
LOUISIANA AVE
DELAWARE AVENUE
MARYLAND AVENUE
Madison Drive
Jefferson Drive
Virginia Avenue
MAINE AVENUE
WASHINGTON STATE AVENUE
L'ENFANT PROMENADE
NORTH CAPITOL STREET
SOUTH CAPITOL STREET
EAST CAPITOL STREET

## CHAPTER 4 – MONUMENTS AND MEMORIALS

itself was not a new design but can be traced back to ancient days when early people built memorials to solar deities (sun gods).

Construction of the monument did not start until 1848, and many, many problems caused it to take longer than had been expected. Delays in getting marble from nearby quarries and problems raising money caused construction to come to a halt. Then a radical political group (called the Know-Nothings) took control of the unfinished monument. They were a prejudiced group who hated Catholics and immigrants to our country. Americans stopped contributing money to the monument because of them.

Construction was again halted when the Civil War broke out. After the War, Congress decided to pay the building costs, and in 1888 the monument was finally completed and opened to the public. That was 40 years after the project had been started.

You can still see the actual place where the construction was interrupted — it is about 150 feet above the base where the coloring of the marble changes.

### DID YOU KNOW?

★ The monument is not as straight as it looks, but gets narrower as it goes up.

★ Some of the marble stones placed inside the monument were gifts to the United States from foreign countries.

★ The Washington Monument is a cenotaph. That means it's a memorial to someone who is buried somewhere else. Do you remember where the father of our country is buried?

---

**MaKe A RE +** 🚌 
(See page 10)

---

👁 _____ The _____

____  _____  _____  _____

**34**

**CHAPTER 5**

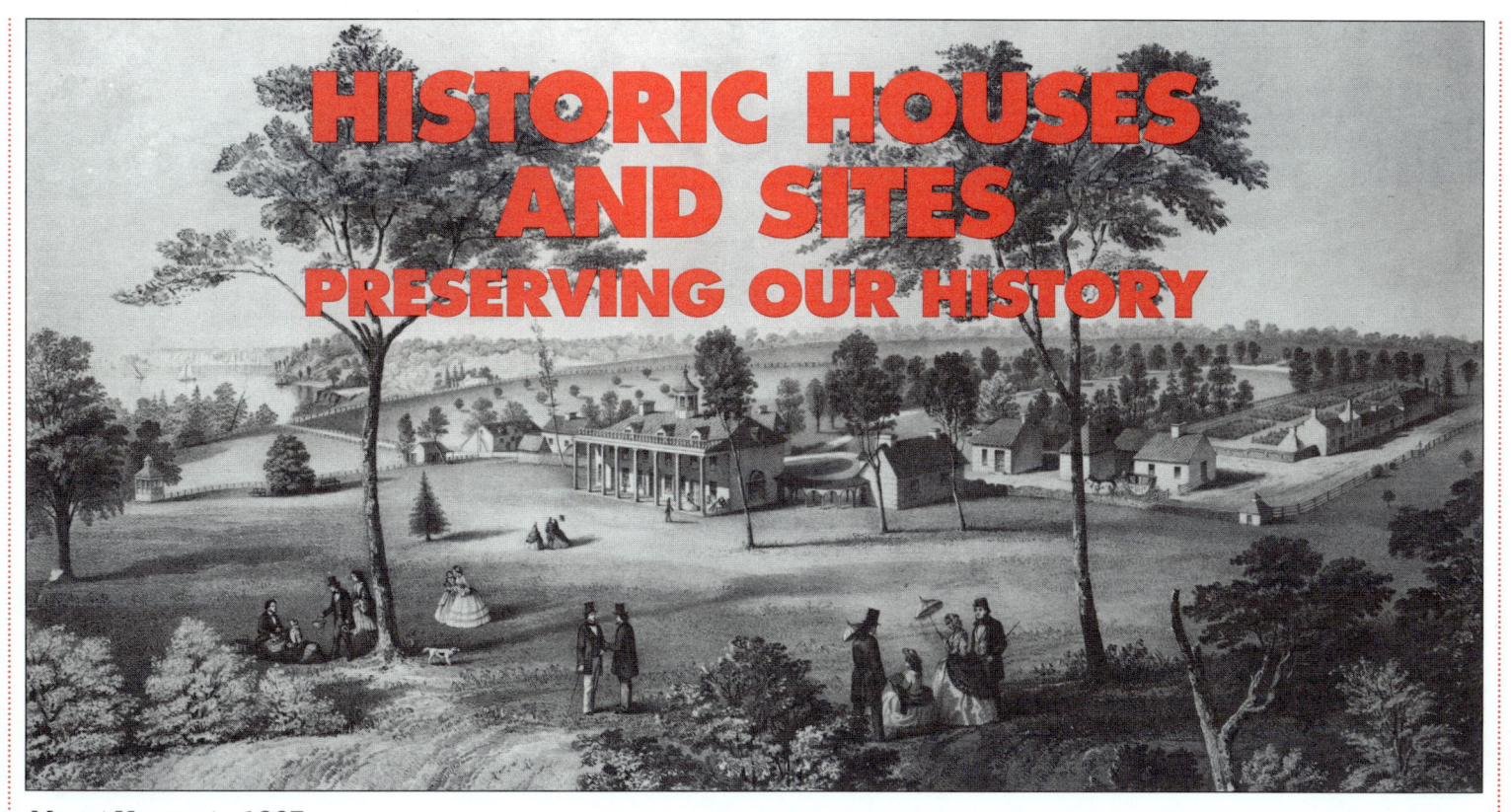

# HISTORIC HOUSES AND SITES
## PRESERVING OUR HISTORY

*Mount Vernon in 1867*

When you tour around Washington — or any historic area — you probably don't realize that much of what you see is because of the efforts of individual citizens who thought our history was worth saving. The reason there is something to see in the Lincoln Museum in the basement of Ford's Theatre is because a man named Osborn Oldroyd assembled many of the items and brought them to Washington. The federal government purchased his collection in 1926, and it was installed in Ford's Theatre. Interestingly, Ford's Theatre itself was not restored and reopened until 1968.

Another example is The Old Post Office, whose clock tower at Pennsylvania Avenue and 12th Street keeps watch over the downtown. A group of people dedicated to preserving the 1899 granite structure fought a successful battle to save the landmark. Because it is so expensive to maintain buildings (particularly older ones), governments often step in to help.

Sometimes though, the job of historic preservation is the work of ordinary citizens. One such group, the Mount Vernon Ladies Association, is responsible for restoring and overseeing George Washington's home.

Entire neighborhoods such as historic Georgetown and Alexandria look much the way they did in the late 1700s because citizens and government work together to make sure the facades (that's the outside) of the buildings remain authentic.

Are there historic buildings in your town? The idea of preserving our history, so that future generations can enjoy and learn from it, is a good one to remember.

## CHAPTER 5—HISTORIC HOUSES AND SITES

### ALEXANDRIA, VIRGINIA
**M** King Street

If you like authentic old towns, spend some time in the section of Alexandria called Old Town. Just across the Potomac River and a few miles south of Washington, Alexandria is the oldest settlement in the capital area. A seventeen-year-old boy named George Washington helped plan the streets of this town in 1749. For one hundred years it was a busy, prosperous shipping port, much like Georgetown was.

Walk around the streets of Old Town Alexandria and look at the many old houses that have been restored to look as they did in the 18th century. You can tour the house where Robert E. Lee lived when he was a boy (607 Oronoco Street) and see the home of George Washington's doctor during the Revolutionary War (210 Duke Street).

### DID YOU KNOW?

★ The *Alexandria Gazette*, which was founded in 1784, is the oldest, continuously-published daily newspaper in the United States.

★ The names of the streets — King, Queen, Duke, Prince, and Princess are reminders of early English colonies in the New World.

### BOXED IN

Each player draws one line connecting two dots (across or up and down).
If you close a square, put your initial inside and go again.
The player who closes the most squares wins.

## CHAPTER 5 – HISTORIC HOUSES AND SITES

You can have a soda at Gadsby's Tavern (Royal and Cameron Streets) where George Washington had his military headquarters during the French and Indian War, and where he celebrated his last birthday.

Be sure to walk down to the waterfront and see the old Torpedo Factory that has been made into an art center. There are many other historic sights to see as you make your way down to the river's edge. Keep your eye out for boats which are still bringing in goods to be sold in Washington, Georgetown, and Alexandria.

### FIND THE ODDBALL

In each of these groups, only three of the people, places, or things are the same. Circle the ONE that doesn't fit with the others.

**1.**
National Museum of American History
National Archives
National Air and Space Museum
Arts and Industries Building

**2.**
Dumbarton Oaks
Renwick Gallery
Botanic Garden
National Arboretum

**3.**
Constitution
Declaration of Independence
Gettysburg Address
Bill of Rights

**4.**
Benjamin Franklin
John Kennedy
Abraham Lincoln
Thomas Jefferson

**5.**
Abigail Adams
Mary Todd Lincoln
Betsy Ross
Martha Custis Washington

*Answers on page 62*

## ARLINGTON HOUSE
(Robert E. Lee Memorial)
Arlington National Cemetery
Arlington, Virginia (703) 557-0613
Daily 9:30 am to 6:00 pm
Closes at 4:30 pm Oct. — Mar.

**M** Arlington Cemetery

When you cross the Arlington Memorial Bridge to Virginia, you can see a stately mansion with columns overlooking the Potomac River. The surrounding land, which is now a national cemetery, was at one time a large estate. The story of the mansion involves two great historical families — the Washington family and the Lee family.

It began in 1778 when John Parke Custis purchased land on the shores of the Potomac. Custis was the stepson of George Washington (he was the son of Martha Custis Washington and her first husband) and served as an aide to the General. He died of camp fever shortly after the British surrendered. George and Martha raised two of his small children, George Washington Parke Custis and Eleanor Custis.

When he grew up, George Custis built a mansion on his father's land. His daughter Mary

*Arlington House*

## CHAPTER 5 – HISTORIC HOUSES AND SITES

### DID YOU KNOW?

★ President Lincoln wanted Robert E. Lee to lead the Northern troops. Lee refused and chose to fight instead for his home state of Virginia.

Anna married Robert E. Lee, a young lieutenant in the army. For thirty years, the Lees lived at Arlington House where they raised seven children. Then something happened which changed their lives forever and prevented them from living in the mansion ever again.

When the Civil War broke out, the U.S. government took over the Arlington estate and used it for an army camp. In the last year of the War, the land that was once alive with crops became a national cemetery for those who had died in service to their country

You can tour inside the mansion which is restored to look as it did in the pre-Civil War days. Walk around the grounds for some dramatic views of Washington across the river. You'll be looking right across at the Lincoln Memorial. It is fitting, in a way, that the mansion faces the memorial — symbols of these two honorable men, Lee and Lincoln, who had fought on opposite sides. Memorial Bridge joins the two memorials and signifies the reunion of the Northern and Southern states.

### CIVIL WAR MIX-UP

Unscramble these words, names, and places.

**ELE** _____
**REVLASY** _____
**CINNOLL** _____
**ONIUN** _____
**SYTRGTEGUB** _____

Answers on page 62

*The C & O Canal*

### CHESAPEAKE AND OHIO CANAL (C & O Canal)

From Georgetown to Cumberland, Maryland
Great Falls Tavern Museum
11710 MacArthur Boulevard
Potomac, Maryland
(301) 299-2026
Daily 9:00 am to 5:00 pm

The Chesapeake and Ohio Canal was begun in 1828 and, when completed in 1850, stretched 184 miles westward to Cumberland, Maryland. For almost one hundred years, rafts, boats, and mule-drawn barges floated up and down the C & O Canal carrying furs, flour, whiskey,

38

## CHAPTER 5–HISTORIC HOUSES AND SITES

If you're interested in finding out more about the history of the C & O Canal, visit the Great Falls Tavern Museum. You'll learn all about the building of the canal and what life was like in the 1800s when boats and barges carried goods to market. You'll also better understand how the locks were used to regulate the water level, so that boats could safely pass through.

Today the canal and the towpath alongside have a new and different use. The canal is a great place to canoe and the towpath is a perfect place for bike riding and hiking. If you really want to experience the old C & O Canal, take a trip on the slow-moving, mule-drawn barge, and imagine how different life must have been in 19th century America. See page 59 for more information.

### CLARA BARTON NATIONAL HISTORIC SITE
5801 Oxford Road
Glen Echo, Maryland
(301) 492-6245
Daily 10:00 am to 5:00 pm
*Tour every hour on the half hour lasting 30 minutes*

Clara Barton is well-known for her role in founding the American Red Cross. While not a nurse, she was a great organizer who saw to it that first aid supplies reached the battle lines to help wounded soldiers during the Civil War. The home that she built, which was also used as Red Cross headquarters, is almost fully restored. You can visit it and learn more about this humanitarian's life and accomplishments.

If you are visiting during the spring and summer, you may want to take a ride on the carousel at nearby Glen Echo Park.

lumber, and coal between Washington and Cumberland.

When the canal was first planned, water was the only means of transporting these kinds of goods. It was natural to think that the busy tobacco port of Georgetown could be connected to the East and growing West by building a canal that stretched to Ohio. But in the next few years, railroads were built for the first time, and it was faster and cheaper to transport goods by railroad than by water. And so the original goal of building a canal from Washington to Ohio was never reached. The usefulness of the canal steadily decreased in the late 1800s, although it continued in operation until 1924.

## CHAPTER 5—HISTORIC HOUSES AND SITES

### FORD'S THEATRE
511 10th Street N.W.
(202) 426-6924 (museum)
Daily 9:00 am to 5:00 pm
*(Theater closed on matinee days, but museum may be reached through side entrance)*
**M** Metro Center

### HOUSE WHERE LINCOLN DIED
516 10th Street N.W. (202) 426-6830
Daily 9:00 am to 5:00 pm
**M** Metro Center

**N**o other theater in the country has the sad history that has made Ford's Theatre a national monument. When President Lincoln arrived to see the play "Our American Cousin" on the night of April 14, 1865, the audience cheered. The band played "Hail to the Chief," and President Lincoln stood at the front of his box to greet the people.

*The Star Saloon*

An hour and a half later, while the play was going on, John Wilkes Booth, a well-known actor, entered the presidential box and shot Abraham Lincoln through the back of his head. Booth then jumped from the box down to the stage. The spur on his boot got caught on a flag hanging from the box. He broke his ankle but still managed to escape. Lincoln was carried, unconscious, to the Petersen House across the street. He died there the next morning.

Ford's Theatre has been restored to look exactly as it did the night Lincoln was shot. In the basement, there is a museum where your can see the clothes the president was wearing, the pistol that Booth used, and the assassin's diary. The museum also has exhibits which describe Lincoln and his life.

From that tragic night until 103 years later, Ford's Theatre was not used as a theater at all. In 1968, the theater was reopened and began once again presenting live plays.

Across the street from the theater, the House Where Lincoln Died has also been restored. You can walk through the house into the bedroom in which he spent his last hours, and pay your respects to one of our greatest presidents.

### Theater & Theatre
Both of these are correct spellings.

# CHAPTER 5—HISTORIC HOUSES AND SITES

## DID YOU KNOW?

★ The box office next door to the theater was the Star Tavern. John Wilkes Booth drank whiskey there just before he shot the president

★ Booth was caught thirteen days after he killed Lincoln. He was found in a barn in Virginia, and when he wouldn't surrender, he was shot to death.

★ Booth was part of a conspiracy to kill Lincoln and other Union leaders. Four of the conspirators were later hanged.

★ On the night he was assassinated, the contents of Lincoln's pockets included spectacles, a pocketknife, a monogrammed handkerchief, and Confederate currency. Does this last item seem odd? Although rarely on display, these items are preserved in the collection of the Library of Congress.

## FREDERICK DOUGLASS NATIONAL HISTORIC SITE

1411 W Street S.E.
(202) 426-5960
Daily 9:00 am to 5:00 pm
Closes at 4:00 pm, October — March

Frederick Douglass was born a slave in 1817. When he was twenty-one years old, he escaped from a plantation in Baltimore and spent the rest of his life fighting to free all oppressed people. He was a writer, a speaker, and a presidential adviser — certainly one of the great African American leaders of the 19th century.

Frederick Douglass lived here from 1877 until he died in 1895. The house, called Cedar Hill, has been restored to look as it did then. The books, paintings, and furniture tell much about this self-educated man and his life.

The tour of Cedar Hill begins at the Visitor Center with a short film that is shown hourly. You will better understand the thoughts and feelings of this great man after reading passages from his autobiography that are on display. His opinions on the struggle for freedom are still very meaningful today.

*Frederick Douglass*

## WHO LIVED WHERE?

*Draw a line from the person's name to the place he lived.*

**Thomas Jefferson**        Cedar Hill
**Robert E. Lee**           Mt. Vernon
**Harry Truman**            Monticello
**George Washington**       Arlington House
**Frederick Douglass**      Blair House

**Answers on page 62**

## CHAPTER 5—HISTORIC HOUSES AND SITES

### GEORGETOWN

You're sure to spend some time in Georgetown on any trip to Washington. If you walk just a block or two from the main streets — with its shops, restaurants, and street life — you'll find that much of the 20th century noise and crowds are gone. You can imagine that you are in the 18th century town of George. Named after King George II of England, George Town (later Georgetown) was established in 1751, long before Washington, D.C. even existed. It became the main port for all of Maryland. A ferry crossed the Potomac River from Virginia to Georgetown carrying such famous travelers as George Washington on his way north from Mount Vernon.

### A Growing Town

Because of its location on the river, it was hoped that Georgetown would become a great commercial center. In fact, it was probably the largest tobacco port in the nation towards the end of the 18th century. Its population was growing. Many Southern families, as well as European immigrants, were moving here. The new capital was being built just across Rock Creek, and Georgetown merchants were becoming wealthy from the foreign goods they were importing and from the tobacco, furs, and lumber they were shipping to Europe.

*Walking the streets of Georgetown*

Large sailing ships were loading and unloading goods daily in the busy harbor between Rock Creek and what is now Key Bridge. But Georgetown's good fortune began to fade with the growth of technology. Steamships took the place of sailing vessels and needed deeper harbors than Georgetown could offer. The Chesapeake and Ohio Canal (C & O) was built to transport goods as far as Cumberland, Maryland, but it couldn't compete with the larger Erie Canal or, more importantly, with the new railroads.

Many of the rich people moved away and Georgetown became an inexpensive and unfashionable place to live. In 1871, Georgetown officially became part of the city of Washington and even its name was taken away.

### Georgetown is Restored

During the 1930's, young Washingtonians working for President Franklin D. Roosevelt were attracted to the former tobacco port. They began buying the old run-down houses and restoring them. Meanwhile some of the larger houses had continued to be well-cared for by local families. Georgetown once again became a source of pride for its residents. A commission was set up to regulate any construction so that the original atmosphere of the community would be preserved.

### DID YOU KNOW?

★ Dumbarton Oaks (3101 R Street N.W.) was the site of a conference in 1944 that led to the creation of the United Nations. Walk through the beautiful gardens, You can understand how problems of world peace might be worked out in this setting.

★ The Old Stone House at 3051 M Street N.W. may be the only house still standing in Washington that was built before the Revolution.

42

# CHAPTER 5 – HISTORIC HOUSES AND SITES

## MOUNT VERNON

George Washington Memorial Parkway
16 miles south of Washington
(703) 780-2000
Daily 8:00 am to 5:00 pm, April — August
Opens at 9:00 am, September — Mar.
Closes at 4:00 pm, November — February
Fee

As a teenager, George Washington often visited his half-brother Lawrence and his wife at their Mount Vernon home. The house, on the shores of the Potomac River, was originally built by George's father. George grew to know and love this land where he rode horses, hunted foxes, and explored the nearby woods and river.

After Lawrence died, George became master of Mount Vernon. He was 22 years old. He and his wife, Martha Custis Washington, lived there until he had to leave to fight in the Revolutionary War and then to serve as the first president of the United States. He returned to Mount Vernon after his two terms in office, but died less than three years later. Washington spent far less time than he would have wished at his beautiful home.

If you take the drive or the boat trip to Mount Vernon, you will have the opportunity to see Washington's home. Remember, Mount Vernon was a full-scale farm. Much that was used on the estate was grown on the land or made here, including fruit, vegetables, meat, shoes, and material for clothing. Mount Vernon covered more than eight thousand acres and was operated by hundreds of workers.

Walk around the gardens, look at the "outbuildings" — the barn, the carriage house (with a carriage inside that's very much like the one Washington owned), the kitchen, and the smokehouse. Take a good look at the house which has been carefully restored to look exactly as it did when Washington lived here — right down to the identical colors of paint and patterns of wallpaper. Much of the furniture you will see actually belonged to George Washington.

*Mount Vernon*

### DID YOU KNOW?

★ Since 1801 every U.S. Navy ship that passes Mount Vernon pays tribute to our first president. It lowers its flag to half-mast, officers and crew salute, and the ship's bell tolls.

★ The names of the two horses George Washington rode during the Revolutionary War were Blueskin and Nelson.

## WOODLAWN PLANTATION

Mount Vernon, Virginia
Route 1, 7 miles south of Alexandria
(703) 780-4000
Daily 9:30 am to 4:30 pm
Fee

The land for this historic plantation was given by George Washington to Nellie Custis Lewis, Martha Washington's granddaughter. It was originally part of the Mount Vernon estate.

The restored mansion and gardens will give you a good idea of early 19th century plantation life. The girls' room looks as though the children were playing just this morning. In the boy's room, you'll find examples of taxidermy (the art of stuffing animals), which was a popular hobby for boys back then.

**CHAPTER 6**

# MUSEUMS AND COLLECTIONS

*Washington Dolls' House and Toy Museum*

**W**ashington is famous for its museums. You may have heard of the Smithsonian Institution, but there are also other important collections here that you may not know about. In fact, there's probably a museum or collection in Washington for every interest or hobby.

The Smithsonian Institution includes 14 museums here, and you'll learn much about science, history, and world cultures from their amazing exhibits. There are also antique doll and toy collections at other places (Washington Dolls' House and Toy Museum and the Daughters of the American Revolution Museum). You can wander around a battleship (Navy Museum), explore nature (Botanic Garden and National Arboretum), or see parchment paper documents from our past (National Archives).

Collections are not only fun to browse through, they are also important for people who do research. Scholars find out more about the present by studying elements of the past. Writers and artists find inspiration. Social scientists are able to trace the course of civilization, and each of us can enjoy learning more about things — great and small — that make up our world.

While you may have a stamp, coin, or baseball card collection or enjoy keeping keychains, postcards, or seashells, you're sure to find new interests to explore. There's so much to see, it can be overwhelming. Remember, you can't see it all on one trip, but you can always come back again and again.

## CHAPTER 6–MUSEUMS AND COLLECTIONS

### CAPITAL CHILDREN'S MUSEUM
800 3rd Street N.E.
(202) 543-8600
Daily 10:00 am to 5:00 pm
Fee
**M** Union Station

**U**nlike other museums, this one is set up JUST for kids. If you're over 14, you may find you have outgrown many of the activities, but you probably would still have a good time if you're with a younger sibling or friend.

Want to try your hand at making music on a computer? Interested in climbing on a police motorcycle or sliding down a real fireman's pole — with hat, coat, boots and all? Curious about the origins of animation and moviemaking and willing to give it a try? If you are, then a stop here is a must. Plan to spend at least two hours.

You can explore a cave dwelling and wander (or crawl) through a room that is actually a maze. Take your turn as a shopkeeper where you can work the cash register while your customers shop. In the Mexican exhibit, you can make (and eat) tortillas and do craft projects too. In another room, you can explore a Mayan pyramid.

On the way in, spend a few minutes in the Nek Chand fantasy garden at the museum's entrance. Its colorful cloth figures and broken tile landscape may give you ideas for projects to do at home.

### DAUGHTERS OF THE AMERICAN REVOLUTION MUSEUM
1776 D Street N.W.
(202) 628-1776
Monday through Friday 10:00 am to 2:45 pm (tour hours)
Sunday 1:00 pm to 5:00 pm
**M** Farragut North or West

**T**ake a peek back into history with a visit here to the many rooms of antique furniture. This is the way houses looked during the founding years of our country. You will probably be most interested in the New Hampshire Toy Attic. You will find a large room with a doll collection and actual toys that children played with in early America. The Touch of Independence Hall includes child-size furniture, a dollhouse, and cubbies with all kinds of colonial objects you can touch and try.

### NAME THAT BUILDING

Do you recognize these famous places?
Write the name of each one underneath the picture.

**Answers on page 62**

## CHAPTER 6—MUSEUMS AND COLLECTIONS

### HOLOCAUST MEMORIAL MUSEUM (UNITED STATES)
100 Raoul Wallenberg Place S.W.
(202)) 488-0400
Daily 10:00 am to 5:30 pm
[M] Smithsonian

The main objective of the United States Holocaust Memorial Museum is to tell the story of the murder of six million Jews and millions of other victims of Nazi rule between 1933 and 1945. During that period, Adolph Hitler and the Nazi Party rose to power and had visions of conquering much of Europe. It was a terrible tragedy.

There are many lessons to be learned from the Holocaust. After a visit here, you will better understand what can happen when people become so fanatical about an idea — be it their country, religion, or way of life — that they are intolerant of anyone who is different or doesn't "fit in." It will make you think about issues such as race and prejudice. It also raises questions about the responsibilities of citizens in one country to those in another.

Because of the subject matter, you (or your parents) may prefer that you tour the special children's section rather than the main exhibits.

If you visit *Daniel's Story: Remember the Children* on the first floor, you will learn about this boy and his family. You will walk through a series of rooms that are designed to look like his house. You will learn how they lived in Germany before the Nazis and what happened to them during the Holocaust. You will understand why this tragedy is called the Holocaust. The term itself means complete destruction.

There is also a Learning Center with a database that can give you more information.

### LIBRARY OF CONGRESS
First Street and Independence Avenue S.E.
(202) 707-5458
Monday through Saturday 8:30 to 5:00 pm
*Call for information on films, tours, and evening hours*
[M] Capitol South

This is the largest library in the world and it is operated by the United States government. When the Library of Congress was established in 1800, it contained several hundred books and maps and was housed in the Capitol building.

After the Library was destroyed by fire in 1814 (during the War of 1812 against England), Thomas Jefferson offered to sell his own personal library collection to the government to begin a new Library of Congress. Jefferson was quite a scholar who had a large and valuable collection of books. Unfortunately, many books were lost in another fire at the Capitol on Christmas Eve 1851. Some books still remain, carefully preserved, at the Library.

The Library of Congress is made up of three buildings called the Madison, Jefferson and Adams Buildings. While most of the exhibits you'll want to see are in the Madison Building, the Jefferson, or main building, is worth visiting for several reasons. Aside from the incredible library collection, the building itself is remarkable in its design and decoration. Outside, notice the carved heads above the second story windows. They represent different ethnic groups from Europe, Asia, Africa, and North and South America.

Once inside the Great Hall, look around you. Look up at the 72-foot-high ceiling and down at the marble floor, inlaid with brass figures of the zodiac, such as Libra and Scorpio. (Can you find your sign?)

## CHAPTER 6–MUSEUMS AND COLLECTIONS

*The Library of Congress*

Millions and millions of items fill the Library of Congress. Besides books, there are mounds of maps, tons of prints, magazines, records and films, and stacks of newspapers that arrive each day from around the world.

The Library serves as an information center for congressmen and senators, students, teachers, and researchers from all over the world. Unlike your library at home, this is a research and reference library rather than one that lends books. You have to be at least 18 years old or a high school graduate to do research here. Some exceptions are made for students who have a letter from their principal saying they have already used all the resources available to them in their hometown. If you ever want to do research here, you also have to have a photo ID with you.

### DID YOU KNOW?

★ There are more than 535 miles of bookshelves in the Library of Congress.

## NATIONAL ARCHIVES

Constitution Avenue and 8th Street N.W.
(202) 501-5402
Daily 10:00 am to 9:00 pm
Closes at 5:30 pm Labor Day — Mar. 31
M  Archives-Navy Memorial

You've probably studied the three documents which form the foundation of our country — the Declaration of Independence, the Constitution, and the Bill of Rights.

You can see them at the National Archives in a glass case at the far end of the main room. Here they are, the originals, handwritten on parchment paper. Even though

*The Declaration of Independence and the Bill of Rights*

they were written two hundred years ago, the ideas expressed are still meaningful today. In fact, the Constitution and the Bill of Rights are being used every day to settle problems concerning how our country should be governed and what our rights as citizens are.

The Declaration of Independence proclaimed the separation of the thirteen colonies from Great Britain and established the United States. It is written on one

**Museums and Collections**

47

# CHAPTER 6—MUSEUMS AND COLLECTIONS

*Thomas Jefferson and the Committee review the Declaration of Independence*

single page and took Thomas Jefferson two weeks to write.

The Constitution is written on five pages (pages one and four are displayed), and you can see the signatures of the delegates to the Constitutional Convention in 1787. The document established the system of the federal government and details the responsibilities of each of the three branches of government — the executive, the legislative, and the judicial. The Constitution begins with the words "We the People," which declare that the powers of the federal government come from the citizens.

A change in the Constitution or an addition is called an amendment. The first ten amendments to the Constitution were added within two years of the signing and are called the Bill of Rights. These set forth the rights of the citizens and include basic freedoms, many of which you have heard about, such as the freedom of every American to worship as he or she wants and the freedom of speech. These are contained in the First Amendment. Today the Constitution contains twenty-six amendments.

Have you ever sat in your school library looking up a word or doing research? Each year thousands of researchers, students, and historians come to the Archives to read documents and records collected by the United States government. Think of the thrill it must be to blow the dust off a 100-year-old document that could help you in writing your paper!

### DID YOU KNOW?

★ The Louisiana Purchase and Abraham Lincoln's Emancipation Proclamation are also in the Archives.

★ For protection the Declaration of Independence and the Constitution are lowered every night into an underground vault.

### I.N.I.T.I.A.L.S.

In Washington you hear a strange language when people are talking about the government — the language of INITIALS.
Find out what these initials stand for.

1. F.T.C. _____
2. C.I.A. _____
3. H.U.D. _____
4. F.D.A. _____
5. F.B.I. _____
6. N.A.S.A. _____
7. D.O.T. _____
8. I.R.S. _____
9. E.P.A. _____
10. N.I.H. _____

**Answers on page 62**

## CHAPTER 6–MUSEUMS AND COLLECTIONS

### NATIONAL GALLERY OF ART
6th Street and Constitution Avenue N.W.
(202) 737-4215
Monday through Saturday 10:00 am to 5:00 pm
Sunday 11:00 am to 6:00 pm (Call for Summer Hours)

[M] Archives

This art museum is made up of two buildings — the original structure (the West Building) and the modern addition called the East Building. The collection is primarily of paintings from Europe and America. In the West Building, you can see early Italian works of the 15th century, Impressionist masters such as Renoir and Cezanne, and works by the 20th century American painter Winslow Homer. In Gallery 6 you'll find a painting by the famous Leonardo da Vinci. Another Gallery has a self-portrait by the great Dutch master Rembrandt.

When you enter the East Building, look up at the huge Calder mobile constantly in motion. Can you spot the giant brightly-colored tapestry by Miro? The large airy lobby leads to smaller galleries on other floors where you can explore wonderful modern art exhibits. When you leave the museum, turn to your left and see how the sides of the building come to a sharp knifelike edge. Isn't the building a work of art too?

Hungry or thirsty? Take a break at the buffet next to the underground passageway that connects the East and West Buildings.

### NAVY MUSEUM
Washington Navy Yard
9th and M Streets S.E.
(202) 433-4882
Monday through Friday 9:00 am to 5:00 pm
Closes at 4:00 pm September — May
Weekends and Holidays 10:00 am to 5:00 pm

Want to climb on a modern ship's cannon, "man" a gundeck, shout "up periscope," and see a model of America's first submarine? Once the home of a Navy fighter plane, this old hangar now houses relics of our nation's naval history. You can learn about the beginnings of the Navy when the English colonists of Massachusetts built the first American warships to fight pirates lurking in the waters off the Atlantic coast. You will see models of ships and learn about how sailors live.

Be sure to save time to tour the U.S.S. Barry — an actual destroyer in its former days, but now

*U.S.S. Barry*

**Draw a Portrait of Your Best Friend.**

## CHAPTER 6—MUSEUMS AND COLLECTIONS

based at the museum. Anchored in the Potomac River, you will be able to walk aboard this battleship that was built to carry 22 officers and 315 men.

While at the Navy Yard, you may also want to visit the **MARINE CORPS MUSEUM** where you can learn more about the history of this branch of our armed services. Exhibits include sample clothing, weapons, documents and photographs.

If you're in the area of the National Archives, you'll be near the **NAVY MEMORIAL AND VISITORS CENTER**, located on Pennsylvania Avenue N.W. between 7th and 9th Streets. Built to honor the men and women of the United States Navy, you'll probably be most interested in the 35-minute film "At Sea," which describes the excitement and adventure of Navy life and is shown, for a fee, on a giant two-story screen. There's also a shop for nautical souvenirs.

The Navy Memorial itself includes a giant granite map of the world on the sidewalk in front of the Visitors Center.

## SMITHSONIAN INSTITUTION

When you're tired of seeing monuments and memorials, it might be a good time for a change of pace and a visit to the museums of the Smithsonian Institution. Unlike most museums you've probably seen, which display paintings and sculpture, these museums contain all kinds of things you've heard about but have never seen.

Remember the moon rock that was brought back to earth by the Apollo 17 mission? Well, that's here and so is the first airplane, gowns worn by former First Ladies, and skeletons of some of the early settlers in the United States — the dinosaurs. The "living" animals at the National Zoo are also a part of the Smithsonian.

The Smithsonian Institution was established in 1846 after an English scientist named James Smithson donated money to the United States government to create an organization for the purpose of increasing knowledge. Today the Smithsonian sponsors research and projects all over the world. And it all started because of the generosity and inspiration of an Englishman who had never actually visited the United States!

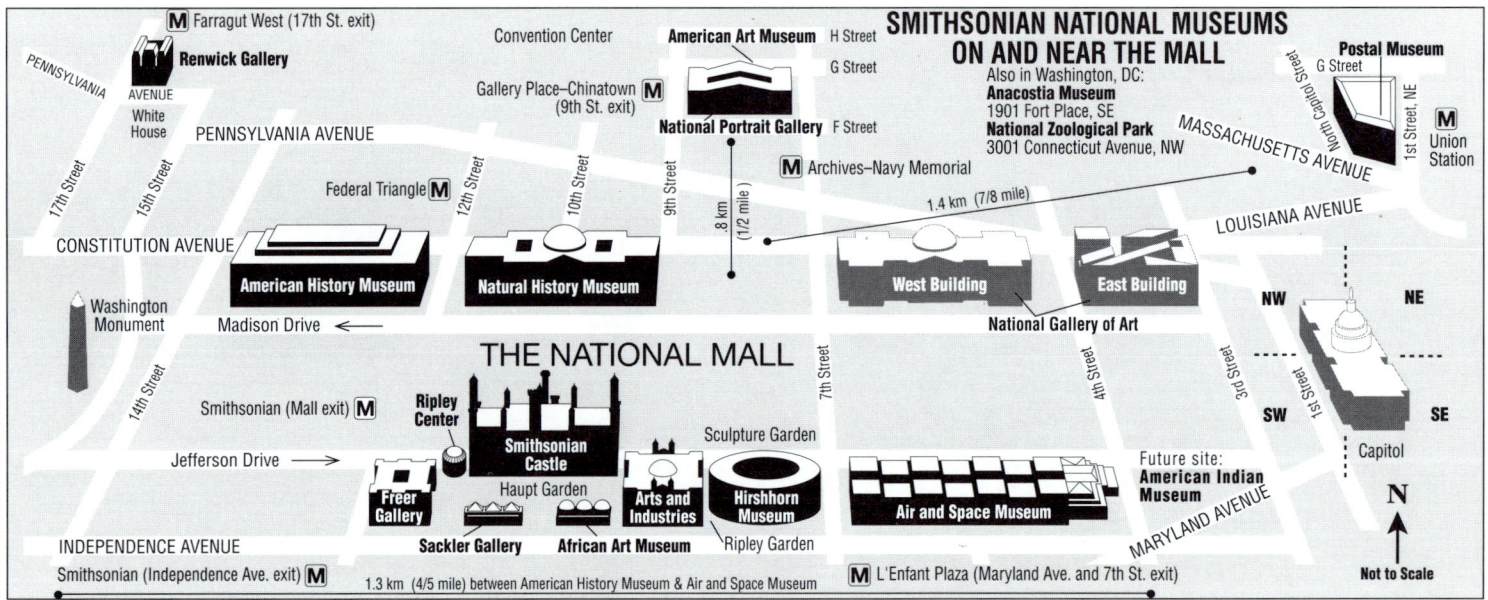

## CHAPTER 6–MUSEUMS AND COLLECTIONS

*Courtesy of the Smithsonian Institution*

The museums are located in several areas of Washington (and also New York City), but many of those you'll be most interested in are on the National Mall. When you visit the Mall area, you'll notice that some of the buildings are very modern, one looks like an ancient Greek temple, and another looks like a medieval castle (the Smithsonian Institution Building). As you walk around, notice the different building styles. Do you have a favorite? You can get some great pictures of the old and the new, and some with the Washington Monument in the background.

Because there is so much to see at the Smithsonian, you may want to visit the Information Center in the Smithsonian Institution Building (the Castle) before you start touring. The Center opens an hour before the museums (9:00 am), and specialists are there till 4:00 pm to answer your questions. A film and several displays describe what's in store for you at the various museums.

An information desk is also conveniently located at each museum's entrance. Stop by to pick up maps, information on current exhibits, and to find out the times of any special programs.

For a 24-hour recorded message about museum programs during your visit, call Dial-a-Museum at (202) 357-2020 (English) or (202) 357-9126 (Spanish). The TTY phone number (202) 357-1729 may be called daily between 9:00 am and 4:00 pm.

If the weather is clear and not too cold, stop between your museum visits and take a ride on an old-fashioned merry-go-round. Pick your favorite horse and close your ears to everything but the music!

### *Smithsonian Institution*
### HIRSHHORN MUSEUM AND SCULPTURE GARDEN
Independence Avenue at 7th Street S.W.
(202) 357-2700
Daily 10:00 am to 5:30 pm
**M** L'Enfant Plaza

**H**uge colorful paintings with bold designs cover the walls of the Hirshhorn Museum. You

**Museums and Collections**

**51**

## CHAPTER 6—MUSEUMS AND COLLECTIONS

can also see figures carved in wood and stone, and others cast in bronze. Some of them will be familiar to you and you will understand what the artist had in mind. Others are not meant to look like any "real" thing and are just beautiful forms in space.

Doesn't the building itself look different from anything you've ever seen? The very modern circular design was made especially so that the painting and sculptures would be easy to view.

Don't forget to wander around the Sculpture Garden outside. There are no flowers in this garden, but many larger-than-life sculptures are "planted" here. Look at all sides of the sculptures and let your imagination go wild figuring out what they could be.

Many of the works here were given by Joseph Hirshhorn who spent years collecting them. Hirshhorn was an immigrant from Europe who came to America when he was a boy. His gift to all of us was a way of saying "thank you" to the country which had been so good to him.

### Smithsonian Institution
# NATIONAL AIR AND SPACE MUSEUM

7th Street and Independence Avenue S.W.
(202) 357-2700
Daily 10:00 am to 5:30 pm
**M** L'Enfant Plaza

*The National Air and Space Museum*

**H**ave you ever watched a bird in flight and wondered what it would be like to soar over buildings and treetops? People have always wanted to fly. The first time someone actually did, he was carried by a giant balloon. Then two bicycle makers from Dayton, Ohio — Orville and Wilbur Wright — made the first successful airplane flight. The Wright 1903 Flyer carried Orville nearly 900 feet. You can see the actual plane hanging in the National Air and Space Museum.

You'll also see the *Spirit of St. Louis*, which Charles Lindbergh piloted on the first nonstop solo flight across the Atlantic Ocean on May 20-21, 1929. He went from New York to Paris, and it only took him 33 hours and 30 minutes!

There are lots of things to see here about our adventures in space. Watch for the *Friendship 7* space capsule, the first spacecraft to orbit the earth. Check out Skylab — the first space station, where three crews of astronauts lived and worked. Save time for the Apollo 11 command module which carried the first astronauts who ever walked on the moon. See the spacesuits the astronauts wore, samples of the food they ate, and an actual moon rock that was brought back to Earth by the Apollo 17 crew. Next time it's a clear night, gaze up at the sky and remember that in Washington you once stood a few feet away

## CHAPTER 6– MUSEUMS AND COLLECTIONS

*Man on the moon*

from a part of that moon. Think about the words of Neil Armstrong when he first set foot on the moon on July 20, 1969: "...one small step for a man, one giant leap for mankind." Plan your visit so that you have 40 minutes to see one of the wonderful films on the theater's giant five-story movie screen. Check the schedule and buy your tickets early as they frequently sell out. You may also want to purchase tickets to see the show in the Planetarium located on the second floor.

If all this space travel makes you hungry, stop in at the cafeteria located on the first floor.

*Smithsonian Institution*

### NATIONAL MUSEUM OF AMERICAN HISTORY

14th Street and Constitution Avenue N.W.
(202) 357-2700
Daily 10:00 am to 5:30 pm
**M** Smithsonian or Federal Triangle

Everything and everyone — from ordinary tools to computers, from ordinary people to presidents — has a history. At this museum you can learn something about the histories of many people and thousands of things. Check at the entrance information desk to find out when the Hands On activity rooms are open, so you can really get a feel for what's going on.

The Foucault Pendulum is one of the first things you'll see when you walk in the museum from the Mall entrance. The pendulum is always moving. Here is actual proof that the earth is rotating. You can watch as the pendulum knocks down the red markers indicating the hours of the day that have passed.

Keep walking and you'll find racing cars, motorcycles, old bicycles with the huge front wheel, and rooms of model ships. If you listen carefully, you can hear the sounds of an old steam locomotive pulling in. You can see gowns that the wives of our presidents wore, cameras from days gone by, and a display that explains the beginnings of electricity.

Telephones, televisions, and computers are probably as much a part of your daily life as sleeping and eating. To get a better idea how this technological wizardry came to be — and how it has changed the world — wander through the *Information Age* exhibition. Check out instantaneous communications and end up in the Control Room where you can see how the exhibition itself is computer operated.

If you sometimes think that science is just a subject that you study in school, think again and explore the exhibits in *Science in American Life*. You'll find out how scientific breakthroughs in one area (such as nuclear advances) have dramatic effects on how we live (underground bomb shelters). You'll find out how technology changed the way our neighborhoods look — with the invention of inexpensive materials that aided the building of less costly houses in the suburbs. And you'll learn more about how we as a society have to make crucial decisions as to how science should be used. You'll even get a chance to try out some experiments in the Hands On Science Center.

## CHAPTER 6—MUSEUMS AND COLLECTIONS

For a return to our past, you may want to stop in at the Hands On History Room. Here you can try your hand at activities and inventions displayed throughout the museum. Sample separating out cotton seeds and you'll appreciate the invention of the cotton gin. Send a communication on a telegraph station and you'll know why it was so important in its day.

Plan your visit so that you are in the middle of the second floor at half past the hour. A huge curtain rolls down and you can see the very same flag that Francis Scott Key saw waving over Fort McHenry during a battle with the British in 1814. On seeing that the "flag was still there" by the "dawn's early light," Key was inspired to write what has become our national anthem. Have you ever thought about the origin of the words in the "Star-Spangled Banner?"

If you're hungry or need a rest, the museum has both a cafeteria and a turn-of-the-century ice cream parlor.

### The Star-Spangled Banner

**W**hat became our National Anthem started out in life as a poem published in the *Baltimore Patriot and Evening Advertiser* under the title "The Defense of Fort McHenry." The tune is not original however. It is a well-known English song, "To Anacreon in Heaven."

For nearly 120 years "The Star-Spangled Banner" was played at important events, but it did not become our anthem until Congress passed an official act in 1931.

Did you know that another of our favorite patriotic tunes is also of English origin? Although written in 1832 by American Samuel F. Smith, the melody of "My Country 'Tis of Thee" is that of the British National Anthem.

*Smithsonian Institution*
### NATIONAL MUSEUM OF NATURAL HISTORY
10th Street and Constitution Avenue N.W.
(202) 357-2700
Daily 10:00 am to 5:30 pm
**M** Smithsonian or Federal Triangle

**W**hen you walk in here from the Mall entrance, you'll be face to face with an eight-ton African bush elephant that is more than thirteen feet tall. Further on, you'll find dinosaur skeletons that have been carefully reassembled. There are also displays about Native Americans and stories of cultures from around the world. You'll also see the world's largest blue diamond — the Hope Diamond. While it is beautiful and valuable, there have always been tales told that whoever owns this diamond will be cursed and have a streak of bad luck.

Be sure to save some time for the Discovery Room. In most museums DO NOT TOUCH is the rule, but in this room touching is required! Here you can "touch and feel" such things as a crocodile head, a woolly mammoth tooth, turtle shells, and fossils.

If you're "into" bugs, stop by at the Insect Zoo where you can see a tarantula being fed and, if you have the urge, pet a cockroach. Check at the information desk at the museum's entrance for tarantula feeding times.

### More Smithsonian Museums...
### ON THE MALL

**I**f you're interested in seeing souvenirs from the 1876 celebration of the 100th anniversary of the signing of the Declaration of Independence, stop in at the **ARTS AND INDUSTRIES**

# CHAPTER 6–MUSEUMS AND COLLECTIONS

**BUILDING**. Much as World's Fairs, Expos, and Epcot Center show us the new technology of our day, the 1876 *Centennial Exposition* in Philadelphia will give you a good idea of one that took place more than a century ago.

After the six-month exhibit, 38 of the 41 exhibitors didn't want to haul their exhibits home, and instead presented them as gifts to the federal government. But where should they go and who should store them? Joseph Henry, Smithsonian secretary, had thought that the Smithsonian would be an institution for study and research — not a museum. Since then, millions of items have been donated by individuals and by businesses. Can you see why the Smithsonian is sometimes referred to as "the nation's attic?" If you look closely above the door to the Arts and Industries Building, it still says "National Museum."

Also located here, the Discovery Theater offers performances for young people October through July. For theater schedule call (202) 357-1500.

A fine collection of art from China, Japan and other parts of the Far and Near East is at the **FREER GALLERY**. The cultures of the Orient come alive at the **ARTHUR M. SACKLER GALLERY**. This museum of near Eastern and Asian art includes objects made for imperial use and others that were made for families to use every day. Many of the objects are ancient and some of the bronzes and carved jades have already survived 5,000 years. The gallery was named for Mr. Sackler, a New York medical researcher, publisher, and art collector who donated 1,000 masterworks of Asian art.

**THE NATIONAL MUSEUM OF AFRICAN ART** is the only national art museum in our country whose main goal is to collect, study, and display African art. You will see carved statues of beautifully polished wood, fabrics that were handmade on all kinds of looms, and pottery of unusual shapes and sizes. You will leave knowing more about daily life on the continent of Africa.

## *More Smithsonian Museums...*
### OFF THE MALL

*Smithsonian Institution*
### ANACOSTIA MUSEUM
1901 Fort Place S.E.
(202) 287-3369
Daily 10:00 am to 5:00 pm

**N**amed for the Native Americans who lived in the area, this museum presents exhibits on the African American experience. History and culture come to life in the exhibitions and programs, many of which focus on the Washington area and its neighboring southern states.

Because the displays are constantly changing, call first or check the newspaper listing to find out about exhibitions being featured during your visit.

*Smithsonian Institution*
### NATIONAL MUSEUM OF AMERICAN ART
8th and G Streets N.W.
(202) 357-2700
Daily 10:00 am to 5:30 pm
[M] Gallery Place-Chinatown

**M**ost of the paintings and sculptures in this museum were created by American artists. You can see works from early times (18th century) right up to the present. You'll be able to see what the United States looked like in the 19th century in paintings by Bierstadt and Catlin.

---

### WORD GAME

How many words can you make using the letters of our first president's name?

## GEORGE WASHINGTON

## CHAPTER 6—MUSEUMS AND COLLECTIONS

*Smithsonian Institution*
### NATIONAL PORTRAIT GALLERY
8th and F Streets N.W.
(202) 357-2700
Daily 10:00 am to 5:30 pm
M   Gallery Place-Chinatown

**T**his museum contains portraits and statues of famous historical people. You'll be able to see how styles of dress have changed over the years by examining what people have worn when they had their portraits painted. The museum also includes the life masks that were made of Abraham Lincoln. Gilbert Stuart's famous portrait of George Washington hangs in the Hall of Presidents.

*Smithsonian Institution*
### NATIONAL POSTAL MUSEUM
First Street and Massachusetts Avenue N.E.
(202) 357-2700
Daily 10:00 am to 5:30 pm
M   Union Station

**I**s there anyone who doesn't like going to the mailbox and finding a letter waiting? Like many things, mail delivery is something you probably take for granted. Especially nowadays with instantaneous communication, most of us find it easier to pick up a telephone to talk than a pen to write a note to a friend – even if the friend lives in another state.

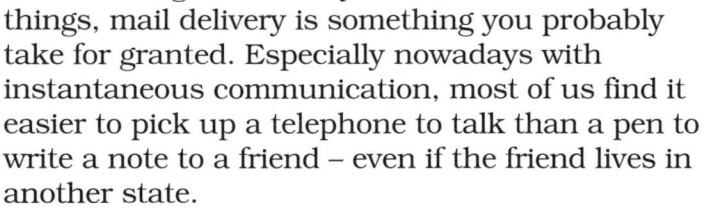

Mail delivery was closely tied to the development of our country, and its history is fascinating to learn about. This museum traces the origins of delivery from the first post rider and Francis Lovelace's (the British governor of New York and New Jersey) attempts to set up regular postal service between New York and Boston. You can follow along a re-created Indian trail similar to that forged between the two cities when postal riders notched trees with their hand axes to mark the 268 miles of their journey. First known as the "King's Best Highway," this passage later became the Boston Post Road. Today that same stretch of road is known as Route 1.

You will learn that overland mail routes helped to encourage more families to move to the unsettled West in the 1850s, because folks would now have a way of staying in touch with relatives back East. You'll be able to design and mail your own postcards; you can view short videos of train wrecks. There are some wonderful homemade mailboxes that may inspire you, and a display of stamps from the world's most complete collection. For you philatelics (that's stamp collectors), there's a stamp store here in addition to a Museum Shop.

## DINNER DILEMMAS

**1.** Not all Washington business is conducted in government buildings; some is done around a dinner table. A Washington hostess was preparing her house for a party. She lost her guest list and could not remember how many place settings she needed. She remembered that when she grouped the guests by twos, there was one left over. If she sat them at tables of threes or fours, there was also one guest left over. But when she sat them at tables for five, they could all be seated. How many place settings did she need in all?

**2.** The bill for dinner at a downtown restaurant came to $200 for 20 dinner guests. The price for each adult was $30. A special price of $20 was offered to senior citizens. Children were charged $5 each. How many adults, senior citizens and children were there?

*Answers on page 62*

56

## CHAPTER 6–MUSEUMS AND COLLECTIONS

*Smithsonian Institution*
### RENWICK GALLERY
Pennsylvania Avenue at 17th Street N.W.
(202) 357-2700
Daily 10:00 am to 5:30 pm
[M] Farragut West

**T**his gallery has special exhibits on American art, design, and crafts. If you want to learn more about crafts, stop by their excellent Museum Shop.

### WASHINGTON DOLLS' HOUSE AND TOY MUSEUM
5236 44th Street N.W.
Chevy Chase, D.C.
(202) 2144-0024
Tuesday through Saturday 10:00 am to 5:00 pm
Sunday noon to 5:00 pm
Fee
[M] Friendship Heights

**B**uy your ticket next to an old post office window and enter a world of long ago: toys of all shapes and sizes, dolls' houses that will amaze you in their detail, and games that your great-great-grandparents might have played.

There are models of French and Spanish schoolrooms along with old-fashioned stores including a hat shop, butcher shop, pharmacy, and grocery. Another room is filled with animal delights — a circus, a zoo, and even Teddy Roosevelt on safari. There are also special exhibits of kitchens from days gone by. Notice the woodburning fireplace. How is this kitchen different from yours at home?

By the way, if you think dolls' houses are only interesting for young girls to play with, think again. Historians and scholars agree that the miniature houses give us clues to what life was like years ago.

## CROSSWORD PUZZLE

**1.** Name the famous bear in the Zoo.

**2.** No. 1 was found in which state? (2 words)

**3.** What regulated the level of water in the C & O Canal?

**4.** Who laid out the streets of Alexandria?

**5.** What is the name of the Japanese island where the most famous news photo of World War II was taken? (2 words)

**6.** What is the name of the president who was also a conservationist and has an island named after him?

**7.** What are the first ten amendments of the Constitution called? (3 words)

**8.** What is the name of the radical group who "captured" the Washington Monument in 1858? (2 words)

**9.** Who was the first man to step foot on the moon?

**Answers on page 62**

*Museums and Collections*

57

**CHAPTER 7**

# OUR NATURAL WORLD

*Botanic Garden*

**W**ashington is a great place for outdoor activities. There are miles of bicycle paths through parks and along the river. You can hike, bike, ride horses, ice skate, row boats, or even cruise on an old-fashioned canal barge.

## BIKING AND HIKING

**C & O Canal Towpath** — If you're ready for a long trip, you can bike the entire 184 miles from Georgetown to Cumberland, Maryland! Or just ride or walk until you get tired, and then stop anywhere along this beautiful route.

**George Washington Parkway** — There are 15 miles of uninterrupted biking along the Potomac River from the Memorial Bridge through Alexandria and on to Mount Vernon.

**Rock Creek Park** — This bike path gets pretty crowded and twisting, but if you're up to it, four miles of biking from Virginia Avenue will take you as far as Pierce Mill. Just beyond are four miles of winding road, which are closed to cars on Sundays.

**Great Falls Park** and **Theodore Roosevelt Island** are also good hiking spots.

## WHERE TO RENT BIKES

**Big Wheel Bikes**
1034 33rd Street N.W.
(202) 337-0254

*Rental rollerblades also available*

**Fletcher's Boat House**
4940 Canal Road N.W.
(202) 244-0461

**58**

# CHAPTER 7–OUR NATURAL WORLD

**Swain's Lock**
On the C & O Canal, 4 miles above Great Falls
(301) 299-9006

**Thompson's Boat House**
Rock Creek Park and Virginia Avenue N.W.
(202) 333-4861

## HORSEBACK RIDING

**Rock Creek Stables**
Military and Glover Roads N.W.
(202) 362-0117.

## ICE SKATING

**National Sculpture Garden**
7th Street and Constitution Avenue N.W.
(202) 371-5340

**Pershing Park**
Pennsylvania Avenue between 14th and 15th Streets N.W.
(202) 737-6937
*Rental skates are available*

## BOATS AND CANOES

**Thompson's Boat House**
Rock Creek Park and Virginia Avenue N.W.
(202) 333-4861

**Jack's Boats**
3500 K Street N.W.
(202) 337-9642

**Fletcher's Boat House**
4940 Canal Road N.W.
(202) 2444-0461

**Swain's Lock**
On the C & O Canal, 4 miles above Great Falls
(301) 299-9006

## OTHER BOATING FUN

**Barge on the C & O Canal**
30th Street and the Canal N.W. (in Georgetown)
(202) 653-5844
*and*
Great Falls Tavern
11710 MacArthur Blvd., Potomac, MD
(301) 299-2026

**Swan Boats (pedal boats)**
Tidal Basin Boat House (by Jefferson Memorial)
(202) 484-0206

**Cruises to Mount Vernon**
Spirit of Washington
Pier 4, 6th and Water Streets S.W.
(202) 554-8000

## BOTANIC GARDEN

1st Street and Maryland Avenue S.W.
(202) 225-8333
Daily 9:00 am to 5:00 pm
[M] Federal Center

Have you ever felt like you were in a tropical jungle one minute and a hot dry desert the next? Surprisingly enough, you can have that unusual experience just a few steps from the Capitol. Inside this glass-covered building, you can wander down paths surrounded by towering palm trees and giant plants. The sounds of a real trickling waterfall make you forget that you are in the center of a big city.

Walk through the huge collection of cactus plants. But don't touch! They have sharp needles all over them. In every season, a different kind of flower collection is on display. You may see azaleas, Easter lilies, tulips, or hundreds of other varieties of brightly-colored flora. This is certainly no ordinary garden!

## CHAPTER 7—OUR NATURAL WORLD

### GREAT FALLS PARK
9200 Old Dominion Drive
Great Falls, Virginia
(703) 285-2966
Daily 8:00 am to dark
Fee

**A**lmost ten miles upstream from Washington, there is a place where the Potomac River drops over fifty feet, creating spectacular roaring waterfalls. Called Great Falls, the scenery is the most beautiful and dramatic in all of Washington. You can get a fantastic view of the waterfalls from the rocks above, but watch your step — it's dangerous here!

The 800-acre park has a Visitors Center where exhibits and movies are shown, and where you can find out information about the falls, the river, and the canal. There are also miles and miles of hiking trails through woods and along the river.

### NATIONAL AQUARIUM
Lower lobby of Department of Commerce
14th Street between Constitution Avenue and E Street N.W.
(202) 482-2825
Daily 9:00 am to 5:00 pm
Fee
[M] Federal Triangle

**S**harks, electric eels, starfish, bass, and sea horses are all alive and well here in Washington. Over 1200 specimens of water life are displayed in living color. If you want to watch the sharks or piranhas being fed, visit the Aquarium at 2:00 pm.

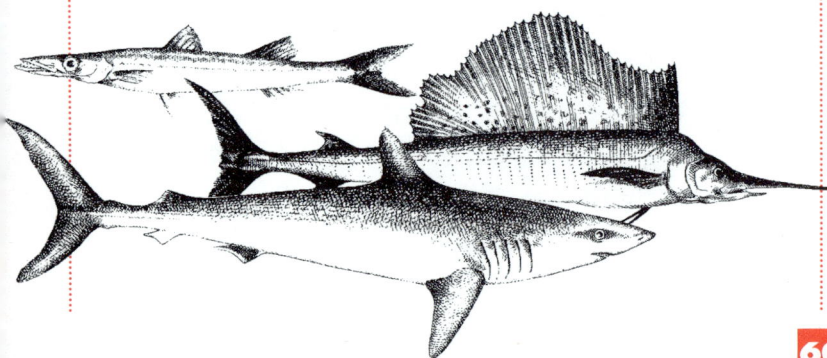

### DID YOU KNOW?
*Some fun fish facts for you.*

✶ The sea horse swims in an upright position.

✶ If a starfish is cut in half, it will grow back into two starfish.

### NATIONAL ARBORETUM
24th and R Streets N.E.
(202) 245-2726
Monday through Friday 8:00 am to 5:00 pm
Saturday and Sunday 10:00 am to 5:00 pm

**Y**ou can walk around the Arboretum all day and still not see all of its 444 acres of trees, flowers, and plants. The main purpose of the Arboretum is to educate people about plant life and to study green growing things.

If you come here in the spring or summer, azaleas, dogwoods, lilies, and many, many other beautiful flowers (whose names are probably not familiar to you) will charm you with their good smells and vibrant colors.

### NATIONAL GEOGRAPHIC SOCIETY (EXPLORERS HALL)
17th and M Streets N.W.
(202) 857-7000
Monday through Saturday and Holidays 9:00 am to 5:00 pm
Sunday 10:00 am to 5:00 pm
[M] Farragut North

**Y**ou've surely seen the National Geographic Society's magazine and school publications, but you probably didn't know that the ideas for all those maps, stories, and wonderful pictures of far away places in the world began here in Washington.

The first floor of the National Geographic Society's headquarters is called Explorers Hall. This is a very special museum where you can explore the world, past and present, through

# CHAPTER 7 – OUR NATURAL WORLD

unique and exciting exhibits.

You can see skulls and bones from man's earliest ancestors and learn about the anthropological work done by the Leakey family. Curious about the weather back home today? You can check it out here at the Real Time Weather station.

Visit the exhibit *Geographica* where you can touch a tornado, experience a rain forest, and amble under a flying dinosaur. You'll learn more about the fragile balance of nature.

The whole world comes together on the largest free-standing globe you've ever seen. It measures 11 feet in diameter. What would you like to explore first?

*Smithsonian Institution*
## NATIONAL ZOOLOGICAL PARK (THE ZOO)
Rock Creek Park
Enter at 3001 Connecticut Avenue N.W.
Harvard Street N.W. or Beach Drive N.W.
(202) 673-4800
Daily 9:00 am to 4:30 pm (Building Hours)
Closes at 4:30 pm September 16 — April 30
M   Woodley Park–Zoo

Elephants, zebras, monkeys, snakes, bats, camels, pelicans and ostriches all reside in the middle of Washington. A great break from sightseeing and museums, plan a visit to the Zoo's three special learning centers where you can touch and learn more about animal life. If you want a really good show, check out the sea lions. They are among the Zoo's best natural "performers."

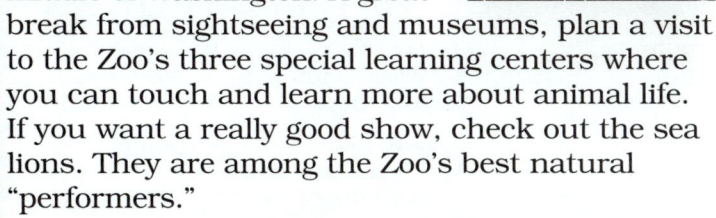

Remember Smokey the Bear? The original Smokey was just a cub when he was rescued by Rangers from a forest fire in New Mexico. Remember what he always says, "Only you can prevent forest fires."

The Zoo is a wonderful place to stroll. There are restaurants and snack stands, but please don't feed the animals!

## THEODORE ROOSEVELT ISLAND
South of Key Bridge in the Potomac River (Off George Washington Memorial Parkway)
(703) 285-2598
Daily 8:00 am to Dark

If you want to get away from the busy city for awhile and spend some time with nature, visit Theodore Roosevelt Island. To get here, you have to walk across a foot bridge from the Virginia side of the Potomac River, because no cars are allowed on this chunk of wilderness.

You'll find miles of trails through this heavily wooded island. Read the markers along your walk and be on the lookout for interesting birds, plants, and small animals. You'll come to a large statue of Theodore Roosevelt, our 26th president and a devoted conservationist. Don't you think this is a fitting memorial?

### MAP TRAP

(Use the centerfold map)

1. What building faces the south side of the F.B.I.?
2. What "body of water" lies between the Lincoln Memorial and the Washington Monument?
3. What building is located due east of the Washington Monument?
4. What street is the White House on?
5. What bridge would you cross to reach Arlington National Cemetery?
6. If you wanted to go north/south, would you use the numbered streets or the lettered streets?
7. What does the D.C. in Washington stand for?

*Answers on page 62*

# ANSWERS

**Page 5: Quick Quiz**
1. President of the United States
2. 555 feet, 5-1/8 inches
3. Potomac River
4. George Washington
5. Alexandria
6. Senate subway
7. Pierre Charles L'Enfant
8. Thomas Jefferson
9. Bureau of Engraving and Printing
10. The Senate and the House of Representatives
11. Ford's Theatre
12. King George II
13. Cherry blossom trees
14. Lifetime term
15. National Archives

**Page 6: Metro Madness**
1. Metro Center or Gallery Place
2. Orange and Blue
3. 17
4. 0
5. 8

**Page 12: Dollar Data**
$1 — George Washington on front, Great Seal of U.S. on back
$2 — Thomas Jefferson on front, Signing of the Declaration of Independence on back
$5 — Abraham Lincoln on front, Lincoln Memorial on back
$10 — Alexander Hamilton on front, U.S. Treasury on back

**Page 12: Coin Crazy**
*Penny* — Abraham Lincoln
*Nickel* — Thomas Jefferson
*Dime* — Franklin D. Roosevelt
*Quarter* — George Washington
*Half Dollar* — John F. Kennedy

The puzzle is worth $3.89.

**Page 17: Find the Clues**
1. Abraham Lincoln
2. Kennedy Center for the Performing Arts
3. Reflecting Pool
4. Tomb of the Unknown Soldier
5. Library of Congress
6. National Museum of African Art
7. Ohio
8. White House

**Crack That Code**
Read the spiral starting from top in a counterclockwise direction. Read the line from the bottom up at the lower left.

**Page 19: True or False**
1. False
2. True
3. False
4. False
5. True
6. True

**Page 19: Washington Search**

```
M W G T H E A T R E I M
L H I R O S U P R E M E
O I F C E N T E R L C M
A T B A P A W R E I A O
G E O R G E T O W N P R
I H U C A T V F R C I I
Z O O H F R O B A O T A
R U T I C O Y I K L O L
T S H V O L R M E N L
A E K E N N E D Y S Y S
S H A S G U O R S O C K
```

**Page 23: Name Game**
1. George Washington
2. Harry S. Truman
3. Theodore Roosevelt
4. Abraham Lincoln
5. Ulysses S. Grant

**Page 23: What Happens Where?**
1. Pentagon
2. Oval Office
3. Capitol
4. Rose Garden
5. The Mall

**Page 23: Nicknames**
1. Dwight Eisenhower
2. Abraham Lincoln
3. William Henry Harrison
4. James Polk
5. Zachary Taylor
6. Franklin Delano Roosevelt

**Page 29: Name That Year**
1. 1776
2. 1812
3. 1865
4. 1871
5. 1865
6. 1793
7. 1800
8. 1863

**Page 31: Name That Noodle**
1. Souls
2. Death
3. Ship
4. Stick
5. Eyes
6. Fight
7. People
8. Thing
9. Truths
10. Country

**Page 37: Find The Oddball**
1. All are part of the Smithsonian Institution except the *National Archives*.
2. All are gardens except the *Renwick Gallery*.
3. All are documents except the *Gettysburg Address*.
4. All were U.S. presidents except *Benjamin Franklin*.
5. All were First Ladies except *Betsy Ross*.

**Page 38: Civil War Mix-Up**
ELE — LEE
REVLASY — SLAVERY
CINNOLL — LINCOLN
ONIUN — UNION
SYTRGTEGUB — GETTYSBURG

**Page 41: Who Lived Where?**
Thomas Jefferson — Monticello
Robert E. Lee — Arlington House
Harry Truman — Blair House
George Washington — Mt. Vernon
Frederick Douglass — Cedar Hill

**Page 45: Name That Building**
1. National Archives
2. Jefferson Memorial
3. The Capitol

**Page 48: I.N.I.T.I.A.L.S.**
1. Federal Trade Commission
2. Central Intelligence Agency
3. Housing and Urban Development
4. Food and Drug Administration
5. Federal Bureau of Investigation
6. National Aeronautics and Space Administration
7. Department of Transportation
8. Internal Revenue Service
9. Environmental Protection Agency
10. National Institutes of Health

**Page 56: Dinner Dilemmas**
1. 25 place settings
2. 1 adult, 5 senior citizens, 14 children

**Page 57: Crossword Puzzle**
1. Smokey
2. New Mexico
3. Locks
4. Washington
5. Iwo Jima
6. Roosevelt
7. Bill of Rights
8. Know Nothings
9. Armstrong

**Page 61: Map Trap**
1. Department of Justice
2. Reflecting Pool
3. The Capitol
4. Pennsylvania Avenue
5. Arlington Memorial Bridge
6. Numbered
7. District of Columbia

*Photo credits:*; **Susan Irwin** pages 2, 3, 18, 26, 27, 28, 29, 37, 40, 47, 58; **Stephen Bluestone** pages 30, 42, 49, 52; **NASA** page 53; **National Park Service** pages 38—39; **Washington Dolls' House and Toy Museum** page 44; **White House** page 21.